To

Keith & Marcia

To Hell and Back...

Anything is possible

Paul

BAREFOOT!

Paul Suggitt
Extreme Adventurer

Paul Suggitt

To Hell and Back
BAREFOOT

www.warcrypress.co.uk

'To Hell and Back - BAREFOOT' ISBN: 978-1-912543-26-7

Copyright © Paul Suggitt 2019

www.paulsuggitt.com

Paul Suggitt has asserted his right to be identified as the author of this work in accordance with the Copyright, Design and Patent Act 1988.

First published in 2019.

'To Hell and Back - BAREFOOT' Produced by Warcry Press on behalf of Paul Suggitt.

Printed and bound in Great Britain by Clays Ltd, UK.

Book cover design by Dan Walker.

Dedication

This book is dedicated to my family for your ongoing patience throughout all my adventures.

Kids, I promise you will get a holiday soon.

It is also dedicated to all who have inspired me along the way, but not the rude bunch of people who demanded I get out of their way in Stonethwaite…I was barefoot and going as fast as I could, you impatient arseholes!

Anything is possible!

Keep up to date with Paul's adventures

www.paulsuggitt.com

@ultraadventurer

Contents

Foreword - Sean Conway

Extreme adventurer and world record holder

"Get these insoles . . . This watch will measure your splits more accurately . . . If you don't wear these compression socks you will die young."

In a world of modern technology and being constantly bombarded with all sorts of things that will most definitely make you run faster, be lighter and remain injury free, it's easy to forget why you wanted to go for a run in the first place.

Taking your shoes off and just going for a run is both metaphorically and physically a stand against the system and makes you feel closer to the earth on which we live.

I know all too well what it feels like to have an idea in the back of your mind that you just have to complete. It sits there giving you sleepless nights and makes your mind wander to all sorts of places you've never been before.

I had this same drive when I decided to run the length of Britain. It was the toughest 6 weeks of my life as I battled storms, snow, midges and stomach issues from severe dehydration. However it remains some of the best memories of my life. Running allows you to travel slowly and absorb the environment around you while giving you time to meet people. It restores your faith in humanity and makes you realise just how wonderful 99.99999% of the world really is.

I didn't run the length of Britain without shoes but when I heard about Paul's barefoot adventure I wish I had. I was immediately drawn to him and his pursuit to prove we are all far more physically and mentally capable than we think we are.

Hear all about Paul's struggle with confidence which eventually led to his 192 mile barefoot adventure across Britain.

Prologue

I still remember the day... Thursday the 18th July 1985, 16 years old and I was called a failure, someone who wouldn't amount to anything in this life, by my dad.

He wanted me to follow in his footsteps and work in ICI, the big chemical giant of the day and without my knowing, he set it up for me to take the selection tests that would lead to interviews and ultimately a job.

It was the done thing back in the day where a son would follow his dad into his line of work, only there was one problem... I had other plans and didn't want to work there.

At an early age, I developed an interest in electronics and the emerging computer world, and this was what excited me and drove my interests, along with girls!

In earlier years at school whilst everyone in the class was making squeezy bottle rockets as their classroom projects, I rocked up with a contraption that initially even baffled my teacher.

It was a block of wood with a ferrous rod glued on to it, a tuner, a crystal earpiece, a diode and a length of wire. Yes my friends, I had made a crystal diode radio receiver that required no power, and despite the teacher not believing it would work, it was great to see her face when she popped the earpiece in and started listening to radio stations like Radio Luxembourg all from my old piece of floorboard and a few components. Win for young Suggs!

The day arrived for me to take this ICI test and I remember being driven to Billingham and being ushered into a room that was the subject of exam conditions. Strangely, I wasn't even nervous going there. I just remember the drive was a non-conversational drive between me and my dad.

The room was dull, grey, dreary, and I looked at the face of every other person in the room, none of whom I recognised and all looking hopeful to pass this stage of the selection process. Why was I feeling different? Was it me seeing it completely wrong? Should I be taking this opportunity seriously?

The exam itself was basic and common sense; however, I knew deep down I didn't want to head into ICI, so I purposely failed the exam.

Thursday the 18th July in 1985 is the day things changed for me forever when the letter dropped through the letterbox informing me I would not be going any further in the recruitment process. I didn't even have time to hide the letter had I wanted to, as my mail was opened for me and the verbal wrath rained down big time, resulting in me being called a failure and that I would amount to nothing in this life.

When I say things changed for me forever on this day, it really did. This verbal battering was all I needed... It was the best motivational kick up the arse ever and my dad didn't realise he did me the greatest favour by over-reacting like this.

I could have took this verbal, voice raised battering on board and become someone in life who would end up being someone he wasn't and begin living life on other people's terms and effectively becoming a sheep, OR, as in my case, I decided what I was hearing was not acceptable and that I wasn't going to just conform to what someone else wanted, regardless if their intentions were meant for my good.

Looking back on this now, my dad eats his words with what happened that day and has seen how I made a successful life. We even laugh about it.

I know his intentions were all good, and he was trying to get me a job at the same place as him, however his way of handling it was the way parents did things back in the day.

I do often wonder how life would have panned out had I taken that other route into ICI... where would I be now? What would I be doing?

Did I make the right decision though? yeah, I sure did... without a doubt.

Not too long after this, and with my fresh awakening on life, I left home and lived at friends' houses and began fending for myself in this big badass world.

My first success came within a year and a half of being told I was a failure whereby I became a manager in a car parts store.

I joined as a sales assistant and my job was entry level, lowest of the low position anyone could have, and primarily entailed sweeping the floors, making the cuppa's, being the butt of the jokes because I was green as grass in an established working environment.

I quickly learnt that being sent for a long stand or to get a box of spark plug gaps was funny... for the other guys.

Was I destined to be sweeping floors the rest of my working life? Was my dad right? Should I have taken the ICI chance I was given? The simple answer was no. I believed in myself from what I now call day 1 of the rest of my life on July the 18th, 1985.

In my head I told myself I would not be sweeping floors the rest of my life and I saw it in my mind, as clear as day, that I would become a manager in that company. Despite the piss takes towards a young green as grass kid, I liked the guys I worked with, and the company itself.

With that in my head, I began taking whatever manuals, company procedure books and product information away with me and began learning the business inside out.

Over the weeks, my product knowledge grew, my confidence with customers grew and so did the respect from my fellow workers.

The result for all this hard work? I became the manager of the store, possibly the youngest manager in the group.

I was now sharing the stage with other retail managers who had worked all their life to get where they were and I was responsible for team members older than me, along with the profitable running of the store.

Was it luck that got me there? No, it was the belief in myself that I could do it and that I was not prepared to sweep floors for the rest of my life and therefore needed to do something about it.

Aged 19 I woke up one day, jumped on a plane and went to Spain to see what it was like and ended up staying there for 2 years. Random? It sure was.

Within days of landing in Spain, I had bagged a job flogging timeshares to British tourists, and I hated every bit of it!

Being told to lie to all the lovely families to try to get sales wasn't my idea of fun in the sun, and despite not throwing the towel in as it is not in my nature to quit, I looked around and found a British company who had set up to help UK ex-pats jump on the Satellite TV bandwagon.

For the next year and a half, I went around rich people's villas and installed satellite dishes on the villa roof's and set up a decoder box that allowed them to receive all the British programmes in Spain.

Sounded glorious? Living the dream at 19? It wasn't, really... In reality, I didn't have a pot to piss in. I was paid barely enough to pay the bills and have a decent meal.

At one point I was so skint I didn't eat for days and ended up drinking the tap water as I couldn't afford any bottled water, resulting in my arse giving way in spectacular style for days.

One thing the job gave me was a decent amount of time off, bringing with it the opportunity to head off into the mountains of Majorca and explore places completely off the beaten track and as far away from tourists as you could get.

My love for adventure was already beginning to grow; I just didn't realise how much of an obsession it would become in my life.

Here I was, 19 years old, in a foreign land, hardly any knowledge of the language, but a thirst and desire to get out there and explore everywhere I could.

Spending time in the mountains ignited something in me that has stayed with me all my life. The sheer tranquillity of nature around me, no humans, no destruction by the said humans and being able to head off with no real agenda was a cool thing to do.

Life simply had no pressure attached to it. It really was uncomplicated.

I tipped up for work, did my job and then I was off into the mountains.

I suppose not earning much money stopped what would have probably been the inevitable of going out and partying with the tourists in Majorca's hotspots every night, which looking back was a blessing in disguise.

After a visit home to see my mates and the offer of a decent job to help kick-start my life back off in the UK, I headed back to Majorca for the last time to pack my essentials up and come back to Blighty.

Cue a big issue!

My passport had just expired, and I hadn't realised. Remember me saying earlier that I took life with ease?

First question then, how did I get out of the UK and back to Spain on it?

This was easy as back in the day you were just waved on by customs and they took no real interest in who you were.

If you wanted a plane ticket from Majorca to the UK, you would visit a known shop on the island and go through a curtain at the back and meet a shady-looking guy who would sell you a one-way ticket to an airport in the country you wanted to fly to.

These were the return part of the tickets people didn't use as they had decided to stay on the island themselves, and work in bars and clubs for the year.

On the last occasion that I had come back to the UK to see my mates, I flew from Majorca to Manchester in the ticket name of Mrs Someone or other. I questioned it at the time and was told no one would check... and the shady guy was right. It didn't stop me from shitting myself though as I checked in and boarded the plane.

We are talking the late 80s here when checks were quite lax.

I didn't want to push my luck any more though with the expired passport issue and had no option but to visit the British Consulate in Palma to help me out.

Easy, right? Well, not really!

I had an official passport application form to fill in, had to get proof from a doctor or other authority on the island that they know me and had known me for a period and to verify that I am who I say I am and then return to the British Consulate with a fee for a passport to be issued on the spot.

Luckily for me (or unluckily for me if you look at it a different way) I knew a doctor on the island. One day whilst in the mountains a dog chased me, and despite running like a madman, the little bastard bit my ankle. A trip to the doctors was now the order of the day.

I seen my Spanish doctor friend and got him to verify who I was, after all, he knew me. 20 quid's worth of Spanish Peseta's later (the days before their currency went to Euro's) and the form was signed, a greasy handshake was exchanged, and I was off on the packed, sweaty bus back to Palma to get my passport.

My memories of this journey to the Consulate centred around the bus driver who sang all the way to Palma and had all his passengers singing away on the route too. I didn't have a clue what they were all singing, but I dived right in and joined them. It was a happy bus.

God knows what they all must have thought... here was a young lad making words up as he went along that made no sense. My arm movements probably didn't help as I funked along to the song.

On this final occasion of leaving Majorca behind, I returned home as a Mr, and not a Mrs, with a ticket purchased from the shady back of the shop guy.

Once home I stayed with the parents for a couple of weeks, however it wasn't long before I left and began kipping at friends' places once again. I left home at 16 for a reason. I wanted my space and independence and being back home wasn't a fit anymore.

By 21 years old I had bought my first house, and once again as a mortgage payer, I didn't have a pot to piss in. I did however have a roof over my head that I could call my own!

Over the years that followed I threw myself into my work, striving to be the best I could be at what I did, whilst trying to get out into the Lake District mountains and lose myself whenever I could. I managed some big companies throughout this period in my life and at one point I was managing a team of over 450 people, so getting into the mountains was a great way to completely disconnect from the long hours and stress of work.

In 1995, my thirst for adventure took another unexpected course, and I combined it with giving something positive back to my community and became a Coastguard Rescue Officer. I was now helping people and still getting the adventure that being part of a Search and Rescue team and thousands of emergency callout situations brought with it over the years that followed.

1995 was also the first time my path crossed with Ian White, who had joined the Coastguard Rescue Service some 6 months before me.

Our friendship connected immediately, and we became the best of mates in a very short time, a friendship that is as strong today as it was back in the day.

I may not see much of Ian compared to a few years ago because of my adventures and training for them, however, our true friendship is one that means when we do catch up, it's like there has been no time gone by since the last catch up. The hangovers are just as brutal as they have ever been as well.

I have promised myself and Ian that after this barefoot adventure; I need to make more time in my life for us to catch up regularly and go out and get drunk, sing songs and have a good old laugh.

On previous big adventures I have involved Ian as part of my support team as much as I could as he is reliable, a shit hot navigator and is prepared to pack in long days like me without it stressing him out. Bring on this latest adventure of mine!

The Barefoot Adventure

Having cycled the Coast to Coast in half a day (12 hours) back in 2016 to see how fast I could push myself in to completing it, and again running it through snow blizzards over the course of 27 hours, across 3 days as the finale to my 2017, 336 day 10,000 mile walk, run, ride challenge; I decided a revisit of the Coast to Coast was in order and to do it in a different and a more extreme way that would test my capabilities beyond that of most human beings.

In early 2017 I met an inspirational adventurer called Paul Burgum and completed the Mercer Surrey Half Marathon with him, (him running the 13.1 miles barefoot) and again later in 2017 our paths crossed after I intercepted him at a place called Orton as he was attempting to cross the country Barefoot. This second meeting with Paul ignited something in me that got me researching barefoot adventuring and led to me figuring out how I could pull off an impossible (or almost impossible) extreme adventure.

In my life I need extreme to push me beyond my comfort zone and even beyond the zone that most human beings would have given up in, and barefoot adventuring seemed to be the perfect fit I was looking for.

The Plan

This was it; The idea was set. I would do the Coast to Coast completely barefoot.

Once the adventure challenge was announced in public it became cast in stone. I do this with every adventure I plan to ensure there is no backing out of it once I have committed to the goal.

Once a goal is set, it is set, and I begin the plan.

So, I'm going to cross the country west to east, totally BAREFOOT, that is all I know at this stage. I know it will be tough, know the start point of St Bees and the finish point of Robin Hood's Bay as this makes up the Coast to Coast start and finish points according to Alfred Wainwright.

The next thing to do is put meat on the bones and work outwards from this point to bring the idea to life.

The first and most important thing was to work out the best time of the year to undertake this adventure. Given it will be slow going, I would need as much daylight as I could get on my side so I could maximise on the time I can walk barefoot, as doing it in the dark, even with the best lighting will be almost impossible and just too dangerous as I needed visibility of what I was taking the next step onto.

June was the obvious choice here as I could start early and finish late each day, allowing me a few pit-stops along the way to rest my feet, and for those times when the terrain would be technical and difficult to get through with no shoes and socks on, without losing any light.

With June the 21st being the longest day, it made sense to actually work that in as my finish day for the adventure challenge and work the days back from there to establish a start date.

My original estimation was this would take approximately 13 days to complete, however the overall adventure would end up finishing after 14 days, so working the days back, I set Saturday June the 8th as the official start date of my barefoot adventure challenge.

With the start date now set 13 months away, I began to study the route itself. It would take me through three spectacular National Parks; the Lake District National Park, the Yorkshire Dales National Park and the splendour of the North Yorkshire Moors National Park.

Having previous experience of adventuring in all these National Parks and knowing the good old English weather is unpredictable at the best of times, I needed to figure out what clothing would be appropriate for this 14-day crossing of the country.

I had to travel light so as to not increase the weight I would put on my bare feet each day across what I predicted to be some horrible terrain. 2 sets of clothing would be appropriate so I could change from one to the other when one set got inevitably wet.

Next thing I set about doing was ordering all the Ordnance Survey maps covering the whole area of the country I was crossing. This ended up being 9 paper maps in total. I embrace the use of modern technology with a handheld GPS navigator and digital OS maps on my phone, however technology can, and does go wrong, so having a fallback of the paper maps was essential for me to continue the adventure and to keep me out of any danger.

With the basic framework set up for the adventure challenge, it was now time to begin the training for it.

Given the extreme nature of this challenge, my feet and mind had to be ready to undertake the brutal daily bashing they were going to get, and whilst 13 months sounds a long time to get on and train for it, as with my previous adventures, the start date soon comes around fast.

First barefoot steps outside of my house (ouch).

We have all been there, having to grab something out of the car and head out of the door and onto the drive barefoot to get it, only to be met with the sudden stabbing pain as we stand on small stones and debris that we haven't seen, and I'm sure we all agree, it bloody hurts.

May 2018 was the first time I took meaningful steps outside on my drive and the road purposely, to get a feel for barefoot adventuring and whether this would really be the next big adventure challenge of mine.

First 1 miler (baby steps to hell)

It's all well and good wandering about on the drive or garden patio to experience the "out of comfort zone" when standing on stones and chippings to try to get my feet used to something different, but this was not going to cut it to condition my feet for a huge adventure challenge like what I had planned in my head.

I needed to get out onto some kind of trail, bite the bullet and take it on the chin (and feet) with whatever happens, just for 1 mile.

I decided that this 1 miler would be my ultimate yes or no point as to whether I proceed with the adventure or plan something different.

I grabbed the ultra-dog to keep me company, made sure I had charged up headphones and a decent playlist to block my head from thinking about the pain, jumped in the car and headed off to Summerhill Country Park and Outdoor Nature Reserve, as it has a mix of trails made up of grass, stones, chippings and dolomite.

The beauty of this Country Park is it is almost on my doorstep, some 2 miles away as the crow flies, and within minutes I can be in the countryside and connecting with nature all around me.

I pulled up in the car park of Summerhill, let the dog out and kicked off my trainers and trainer socks, left them in the car's footwell, took a deep breath and took my first proper public barefoot steps.

Talk about toe curling times... it bloody hurt!

I had to stand there for a good couple of minutes while my feet became accustomed to this new experience and for my mind to stop being pissed off with me for putting it through this sudden pain, especially as it knew I had trainers in the car.

The idea of leaving my trainers behind was simple, it would force me to complete this 1-mile test without the temptation of putting my shoes on if I was carrying them with me.

This is exactly the mentality I had on the actual barefoot adventure challenge... taking no footwear with me.

I have to admit, this first mile wasn't fun at all and it took a strong mind to push through the varying degrees of pain I experienced.

What did I take away from this first mile test of barefoot walking?

Firstly, it confirmed I am crazy!

Secondly, it showed that no matter how much it hurt my feet; I completed what I set out to do, even though it was only 1 mile. Baby steps to Hell!

Third, it forced me to look for what I call "quick wins", finding patches of grass wherever I could, no matter how small they were, to help take the pain off my feet temporarily. Why walk on the sharp rocky terrain when there was grass alongside it?

This was the adopted procedure on the challenge itself, looking for "quick wins" wherever I could.

First 5 miler

After the success of my first 1 miler and understanding the type of pain I was going to facing and experience on my barefoot adventure, I was ready to push 1 mile into 5 miles, varying the terrain as I went along.

Setting off from my house with the ultra-dog, I headed off through West Park on a mixture of pavement and grass, till I came to the trails that led off to Summerhill Country Park and then to Dalton Piercy.

These trails were a mix of grass, mud and stone, perfect for simulating some trails I would come across on my big adventure.

Heading out to Dalton Piercy the trails were awash with overgrown nettles, thistles and brambles, however, the ultra-dog was helping me out by running through them as if nothing was wrong, so I followed in her footsteps (or paw steps) to help get me through these patches of overgrown nasties with minimum impact to my legs that were getting a beating up with the nettle stings and bramble scratches.

I've never figured out the purpose of a nettle, apart from the fact I can boil it up into a tea or it can really piss you off when stung by one. Other than this, I do not understand the purpose of a nettle.

Walking along the duck board to the access gate on to the road at Dalton Piercy was an experience for the ultra-dog.

She had seen nothing like it before so did an army crawl across it while I was trying to coax her to the gate so we could continue into Dalton Piercy and then back on the trail to intercept Summerhill Country Park once again.

Once the dog had sorted herself out, we were back en route to Summerhill, through more nettles, some as tall as me at this point.

Crossing farmland and the slurry that came with it we were soon at the "tin man" of Summerhill and the terrain had changed back to that of what I experienced on my first 1-mile walk. This part of the walk was probably the most painful as the trail was made up of fine and often sharp stones, so I began to look for quick wins of bits of grass to balance the pain out with a bit of relief here and there.

Once back home I had a shower and began to feel a funny sensation in the base of my feet. Something didn't feel right. I looked at the bottom of my feet to find them awash with small thorns embedded in them.

I tried squeezing these little suckers out of my feet, but to no avail, so the search was now on for a pair of tweezers. After 20 mins of pulling these small thorns out of my feet, they began to feel normal again.

Note to self, add tweezers to the kit list for the barefoot adventure.

First 10 miler

Building on what I had learnt from my 5-mile jaunt around the trails on the outskirts of Hartlepool, it was time to actually head out and increase the mileage under bare foot.

This time, the terrain had to have some real connection to what I would come up against on my adventure challenge. I needed the rugged paths, the steep hills, the grass, the stones, and whatever else could knock me out of my comfort zone.

Where could I get all of this? Why the Cleveland Hills of course and only a 40-minute car ride away.

This was also the perfect opportunity to get some familiarisation in with the handheld GPS and the OS mapping on my phone. For good measure, I brought along a paper copy of OL26 Ordnance Survey map as my backup in case the tech failed.

After checking the weather, I prepared a small backpack with energy bars, hydration drinks, GPS tech, threw the hound in the car and I was off for the drive to my starting point of Clay Bank.

I chose this start point as I would cross this area for real on my barefoot adventure challenge. After parking the car up, ditching my trainers and gingerly walking up the bit of road to the gate that led me up Carr Ridge and onto Urra Moor, it suddenly threw me out of my comfort zone. "Oh, my fucking god!" the instant pain in my feet hit me like a train.

I began focussing heavily on the ground ahead of me, walking on the big flat stones embedded into the trail and looking for the quick wins the grassy area could bring me as I zigzagged around the nasty bits.

Once on the top of the moor after battling the pain of these first steps on "very real" terrain, I took a pit stop and fired up the GPS.

My thoughts soon turned to the challenge that lay ahead of me... Had I bit off more than I could chew here? Is this 10-mile circuit of the Cleveland Hills going to finish me off?... am I crazy? (Er yes!)

Watching the ultra-dog take every step in her stride, I was envious... "if only my feet could be padded right now like hers are," I began thinking.

Normally walking these beautiful hills helps me get away from everything, however today I was finding it difficult to see anything beautiful about the situation I had put myself in. This walk was testing my whole strength and resolve as I crossed the moorland and back to the car.

What would have taken me a few hours to walk in hiking boots ended up taking me the best part of 8 hours to do in bare feet, putting me on an average speed of 1.2 miles an hour. I was beating myself up over this, not realising that this would become a "normal" average speed on the challenge itself.

Driving back to Hartlepool I was reflecting on the whole day. Should I scrap the challenge? Is it beyond me?

By now, the pain in my feet was subsiding and with it any thoughts of quitting. I just needed to keep working at this and toughening my feet up to ride out the pain.

First 15 miler

My first 15 miler barefoot walk came courtesy of an initiative by Hartlepool Borough Council who were keen to promote their clean streets initiative, so what better way to do this than with a lunatic in a crazy hat walking barefoot for 15 miles around the town?

I started off at Radio Hartlepool on York Road and headed out along York Road and the town centre, down to the marina, along the promenade to Seaton Carew, up to and around Owton Manor, along to West Park, Throston, Central Estate, The Headland and all the way back to where I started.

It took 5 hours to complete and was a total of 15 miles.

The great thing here was I only came across 3 lots of dog shit the whole way! For a barefoot guy, this is an important thing!

At one point, I was intercepted by the Police, who were initially concerned for my welfare. I wonder why?

As I came to the junction of Holdforth Road and Winterbottom Avenue (Just past the University Hospital of Hartlepool) the Police were staring at me from their patrol car, so I gave them a thumbs up and carried on walking.

By the time I had crossed the road they had spun their car around and came running on foot through the path from the trading estate to the main road I was on, shouting to me "Is everything OK?".

I assured the officers that all was fine and that I was an adventurer who was combining his barefoot training with an initiative by Hartlepool Borough Council.

God knows what they must have thought on first appearances... here is a guy wandering the streets in a crazy hat and no shoes and socks on... of course they would pull me over... they couldn't let that one go could they?

After a bit of banter and the constables sticking a thumbs up on my social media posts about the day, I was back off on my barefoot travels.

With the positive comes the negative, and this day was a tale of both sides, courtesy of white van man, parked up at Throston, an area of Hartlepool I had just passed through.

Walking down the road I saw a white van full of lads ahead of me and as I approached them, I was trying to look inconspicuous in a crazy hat and bare feet... I was thinking "please don't acknowledge me, please don't acknowledge me..." damn! they noticed me and shouted me over, asked me what I was doing in the hat and bare feet and then flicked 2p at me and told me to "fuck off you dick head".. nice chaps... not!

Strengthening my feet up

Feet aren't just weird; they are essential body parts that are also very sensitive, feeling everything they come into contact with.

In fact, one of the most sensitive parts of the body is the soles of the feet. This is because the foot has a high concentration of nerve endings, some 200,000 of them per foot.

The arch is the more sensitive part of the foot with the skin almost wafer thin and the nerve endings are much closer to the surface, meaning it doesn't take much to hurt them compared to the heel or the ball of the foot, as these two parts take the impact of walking day after day so they are a lot more hardened up in general.

My feet strengthening consisted of daily walking on various types of terrain to accustom my feet to the different feelings it brought with it, along with using a Shakti mat to help my mind and body become used to the pain.

Strengthening my mind up

It's not just about strengthening my feet up; I need a strong mind to go with it as well so they can work in unison. This applies to all my adventure challenges. I have to have the right mindset, as all extreme challenges have the potential to put an adventurer into a dark place. The constant battle against the elements, terrain, and isolation can really take its toll.

Having first-hand experience of dark places on previous adventures, I took consideration from the outset as to how this extreme adventure would play out in my mind.

I had pain to deal with, not just in my feet but in my mind too. I had the elements to deal with; I had the difficult terrain to deal with. All these things have some kind of negative impact attached to them and it's crucial I could manage them all positively.

One thing I have had the ability of since being a teenager is being able to visualise a positive end result to something in order to achieve it. This has applied to all areas of my life, from learning to drive, learning to fly and through to all my adventures over the last few years.

Seeing myself at the finish of a tough adventure, feeling the elation at having completed the almost impossible, experiencing the location, the people congratulating me, it all serves as a way of embedding the success of the task in my mind.

By doing this, I create a belief in me that my end goal is achievable. It may be difficult along the way, but totally achievable.

By accepting that unplanned things will happen, and to get on and deal with these things will help me embrace the success in my mind.

All I have to then, in reality, is figure out each day of the adventure for real. By now, in my head, I know I will complete the challenge at all costs as I have seen the end result in my head and my mind has now registered it as a real event.

It is a proven strategy that has seen me achieve a lot of things in this life, not just with my adventuring.

Strengthening my knee injury up

Since completing my big 10,000-mile walk, run and ride adventure challenge back in 2017, I have suffered with an area of my left upper leg that runs from my hip, down to my knee that is totally dead. It is an area of about 1cm in width, running down the length of my thigh and it literally has no feeling whatsoever.

The other injury I picked up is on my left knee itself and it is a bit buggered from all the running I did throughout the 10,000 miles and 336 days.

Given the extreme nature of the barefoot challenge that lay ahead of me and the fact I would rely on a pair of legs that actually work to have any chance of completing it, I needed to get a strengthening plan set up to bring my legs back to a fit working state.

After many visits to the doctors, painkillers and visits to the physio, it was Ian Glass from Ian Glass Fitness who realised what was happening with my leg, identified there was muscle beginning to deteriorate and he created a strength training program focussed on this area to help me make a great recovery in time for my barefoot adventure. This wasn't an overnight process given the damage I had inflicted on myself from previous adventures, however after 6 months of determination and effort to get this sorted, and the benefits of barefoot walking, it saw me become "adventure ready" for June 2019.

Daily training

Keeping up a daily training regime for my feet was so important in order for them to continue to get used to the pain and terrain to prepare for my barefoot adventure.

Daily training included a minimum 2-mile barefoot walk with the ultra-dog, much longer at weekends and on training weeks away, and sessions on my Shakti mat. A Shakti mat is a yoga type mat that resembles a bed of nails. It is in fact a mat with

6,200 pointy bits sticking out and is made primarily for someone to lie on, however; I used it as a way of conditioning my feet. Given the nature of the design, it would not puncture the skin on a persons back or feet, but boy did it hurt.

A typical session on the Shakti mat lasted around 20 minutes where I would stand on it barefoot with my full weight for a few minutes and then walk on the spot on it for the rest of the session. This simulated the sharp scree I was to encounter on my adventure and helped my feet (and mind) prepare for this.

Daily training for 13 months helped my feet toughen up so much, with the balls of my feet and heels becoming thicker with the tough skin forming in these impact places.

Kit preparation

Ensuring I have the right kit for the type of adventure I am undertaking is so important, and it is a process that begins not long after the idea for the adventure is born.

I give consideration to the location I am adventuring in, the likely weather I will encounter en route, the type of adventure I am undertaking (walking, running, riding, climbing), the time of the year, etc.

Having had the benefit of prior experience of the Coast to Coast from past adventures, I knew the terrain I would operate in on this next big barefoot challenge.

Given I was walking one side of England to the other, through mountains, hills, trails, and knowing how England is wet at the best of times, I needed to make sure I had kit that would protect me from the elements.

Normally this would include appropriate footwear, however, on this particular adventure footwear was not needed.

My kit comprised of:

1 Crazy hat

2 Beanie hats

1 Pair of sunglasses

1 Pair of gloves

2 Water Bottles

1 Walking Pole

2 Lightweight waterproof jackets.

2 Fast wicking T-shirts.

2 Pairs of shorts.

1 Pair of leggings.

9 Ordnance Survey paper maps covering the whole adventure.

1 Handheld GPS navigation device.

1 Subscription of OS digital mapping.

1 Satellite tracker.

2 Portable backup batteries.

1 First aid kit.

4 Packs of wet wipes.
Support team

On all of my adventures when not going at them solo, I have a support team helping wherever they can.

My support team can sometimes be 1 person who gets me to the start of an adventure and picks me up at the other end or be around some days to ensure I have maps ready for the next day, charging my kit up for me and so on.

Sometimes I have more than 1 support person, as with my barefoot adventure. Support on this adventure came in the form of Mick Jorgeson and Ian White, with additional support from Documentary Filmmaker, Dan Walker who was there to film the challenge.

Ian was to accompany me on my daily walking, and capture film footage from the mountains and trails for Dan. Ian had expressed an interest to do this as he has always wanted to complete the Coast to Coast and given one of his family members had just come through cancer, he also took the opportunity of attempting it to raise some money for cancer research along the way.

Many people intercept me on my adventures as I share my location and progress via my satellite tracker, however, having Ian come with me, even if it was to film my progress, was a godsend.

13 months came around quickly, and the time had now come to travel over to St Bees and get ready for this epic barefoot challenge.

Let's do this!

Day 1

St Bees to Ennerdale Bridge

I travelled to St Bees the evening before my challenge and sat in silence most of the way as I weighed up the weather and how it appeared to be getting worse the closer I was getting to the west coast.

I studied the met Office app on my phone but no matter how many times I looked at it, the weather report wasn't getting any better. I just had to accept the fact that I would start my challenge in some of the worst June weather England would experience for a long time.

Once in St Bees I, along with Ian and the support team made a hasty dash up the road so as not to get soaked with the rain, to the Manor House pub to have a few beers and a bit of banter.

St Bees is a special place to me and holds fond memories of being one of my stop off places on my 2017 10,000 mile walk, run, ride adventure challenge. Back in 2017 I put an appeal out on social media for anyone who could put me up for the night in either Whitehaven or St Bees as I completed a leg of my challenge from Gretna Green to Barrow in Furness on the bike. I could have slept under my trusty tarpaulin for the night but needed a roof over my head for a change and a decent shower.

After thousands of social media shares, someone who I will refer to as my "canny stranger" came on the radar and offered to put me up. Modest to this day, she won't let me use her real name, but what a great person she is.

I had a support team with me on this leg of my 2017 adventure as they were heading over that way anyway and shadowed me here and there, and this too wasn't a problem for them to crash at my canny stranger's house too. The only condition was I had the spare bedroom to myself and they kipped on the sofa. I needed my space!

That night resulted in what I can only describe as a total bender and I was dreading setting the satellite tracker away and heading off on the next leg of my challenge the next morning.

That adventure is for another book and I will just say that it was one of the best nights out I have ever had over on the west coast!

Back to this occasion in St Bee's, this time I took it easy on the alcohol and after a couple of pints and a bag of the obligatory pork scratchings in the Manor House; it was time to head back to the railway station car park and get my head down for a few hours.

Overnight, the predicted storm I was monitoring on the Met Office app made landfall with a vengeance and battered the hell out of St Bees.

On waking up early because of the torrential rain, I wandered over to the support vehicle for a cup of coffee and a bit of banter with the lads. As it was pouring down with rain, I had no option but to step out of the wet and into their lair and it was a typical man smelling, early morning musky cave.

I still couldn't believe it; this was the day it was all happening. Today I take the first barefoot steps on a challenge that will take me 2 weeks and a distance of 192 miles to complete. 13 months ago this was just an idea, now here I was casually having a laugh with the support team prior to being driven the 1 mile to St Bees Beachfront Car Park.

I was excited but very nervous at the same time.

On parking up at the Beachfront Car Park, I began to get ready for the day ahead, checking the weather forecast again and predicting the gear to take with me en route to Ennerdale Water, some 15 miles away.

The weather was worsening by the minute and the west coast out to sea was looking very gloomy. It was dull and very grey, and the tempests were angry. The sea was like a cauldron bubbling and frothing, and the rain stung my face as it drove into me like needles being fired at speed. At points I felt my breath being ripped out of me with the power of the wind.

Whilst in the support vehicle putting my signature hat on and rubbing some potions into my feet to keep them subtle from the outset of the adventure, the folks from the Chris Lucas Trust arrived in the car park.

I was excited to see Lynn Lucas, her husband, also called Lynn, and some great friends from the Chris Lucas Trust, a charity I have supported for many years and one of 2 charities I am raising awareness and funds for on this barefoot adventure of mine. They all arrived in St Bees last night too and came to meet me for the start of my challenge.

When I popped my head out of the door of the support vehicle, I saw a whopping big banner with my head on it. It didn't stop there; all the girls had a crazy hat on as well in solidarity to me and my crazy signature head piece. What a feel-good factor this gave me and an incredible and powerful boost to the start of 2 weeks of unknown.

After a few pictures with the charity to capture the moment, it was soon 9am and my official start time for the adventure to begin.

With this, I powered on the satellite tracker so everyone at home and around the world could begin watching my progress as I took those first steps into the great unknown. The next time I would see all the lovely people from the Chris Lucas Trust would be in two weeks' time at the end point of my challenge, Robin Hood's Bay.

The very start of the crossing of the country saw me tap the Coast to Coast monument at St Bees twice for good luck and then I was off on my epic barefoot adventure.

Being a Saturday and a traditional day to start the Coast to Coast; there were quite a few groups of hikers on guided hikes, individuals and couples all setting off to begin their own adventure, sensibly though with boots on their feet.

Heading up the hill to get onto the tops at St Bees Head, the weather battered me. The rain was so heavy, and the

26

wind was driving it into me with great force. Within minutes it soaked me to the bone and those feelings of having the breath ripped out of me were even worse the higher I went.

So far up the route to the top of St Bees Head, I had to find a place to shelter as I was due to take part in an interview with BBC Radio Cumbria at 20 past 9 and storm Miguel was absolutely raging around me.

Being on an exposed hill there was no chance of real shelter so I had to go off the path that led up St Bees Head and tuck myself away into the corner of the field where I crouched down near a gorse bush for shelter, pulled my hood as far over my face as I could, trapped my hand and phone in there with me and hoped the interview would go without a hitch. Today saw the UK on track for one of the wettest June's on record. Bloody typical.

I wasn't aware of this at the time of the live interview with the BBC, however, a herd of cows had half circled behind me whilst I was crouching down sheltering as best I could out of the storm so I could try to have as normal a chat with the presenter on the radio. It is just as well I didn't know this as I don't like cows and had I known they were surrounding me I would have totally freaked out. No doubt it would have made good listening and a great comedy value to everyone on the other end though.

Walking round the head at St Bees saw me ankle deep in water as the ground couldn't take the amount of rain being dumped on it and it began to flood. This created a rapid cooling and withering effect on my feet, making them appear like I was experiencing the onset of trench foot.

Once clear of St Bees Head, the weather broke temporarily, allowing some sunshine to poke its nose out of the clouds and brighten things up. I took a pit stop at a place called Sandwith and it is here I met Andy Lindsay for the first. Andy had heard I was doing the Coast to Coast barefoot and wanted to catch up with me. The timing couldn't have been worse though.

I think the nerves of the day had caused me to get a dodgy belly and thankfully on arriving at Sandwith; I saw my support vehicle parked up there with Mick hanging out of the door with a cup of coffee ready to go for me. I rushed up to the van and took residence on the onboard toilet, breathing a huge sigh of relief.

Being a guy and not giving a shit, well in this case maybe that's the wrong phraseology to use, but when Andy shouted through to me that he was outside, I began chatting to him from inside the trap, not realising there were another half a dozen people with him at that point.

Once I had sorted myself out, washed my hands and picked up my much needed cup of coffee, I wandered outside of the support vehicle to meet Andy face to face, have a chat with him and have my photo took with the group of people he was with.

This was Andy's 5th crossing of the Coast to Coast, so I probed him for tips and any other advice he could give me. Andy is one of life's good guys and a real gentleman.

With time ticking on, and wanting to take advantage of this break in the weather, I headed off from Sandwith and en route for Cleator Moor. Along the way the forestry commission had closed roads and paths associated with the Coast to Coast, and they put diversions in place for walkers.

Under normal circumstances these diversions would be welcomed by someone in hiking boots, but given I wasn't wearing anything on my feet and the diversions routed us onto freshly laid stone chipping roads with no grass verges for miles, this created an instant impact on my average miles per hour and the pain was off the scale with each step I took.

This was the first real hard impact on my feet since I started at 9am, and I wasn't liking it one bit. I had no control over the obscenities coming out of my mouth. It felt like I was walking on knives with every step I took. Still, I was making progress with each step I took and my end goal today was Ennerdale Water.

To get there, I walked through Ennerdale Bridge and almost called it a day there as after the big diversion by the Forestry Commission and the sudden change in unfriendly terrain, my feet were really feeling the pain.

At Ennerdale Bridge I took the opportunity of looking at the map and saw my end goal was only 1 mile away. My choice was either do this last mile now and start from Ennerdale Water tomorrow or call it a day here and add an extra mile onto tomorrows daily mileage.

Given there was loads of daylight left and still juice in my feet despite them hurting, I opted for continuing on to the start of Ennerdale Water so I could begin there tomorrow.

The local pub, the Fox and Hounds was a charming and busy pub that served up great grub and a lovely pint. The landlord was a spot-on bloke who even sent my table a round of drinks over, on the house. The locals were equally nice, taking time out of their night to chat to me, ask me how my first day was and whether I was continuing on with the challenge or having a rethink.

Word was also beginning to spread among hikers that there was a "crazy hat" wearing guy doing the Coast to Coast in his bare feet. Chatting over food with two Canadians on the next table who were also crossing the country, they mentioned that they had heard about my adventure and were absolutely gob smacked at my plans to be doing the whole route barefoot.

After a couple more beers with locals and hikers doing the Coast to Coast, it was time to get my head down and grab a few hours' sleep as despite day 1 now being boxed off and my overall mind and body feeling good; I wasn't kidding myself that there was still a very long way to go.

This was the first day of two weeks completed and tomorrow the fun really starts as I head on to a lot more challenging terrain and head off into the mountains.

Day 2

Ennerdale Bridge to Honister Slate Mine

My feet were feeling good considering I had completed 15 miles barefoot yesterday; however, I wasn't about to count my chickens and kid myself that every day will be like this. Yesterday was the easy day, and I knew that. Today is the day I enter the mountains, and as a man of the mountains, I knew what was ahead of me.

After a cup of coffee whilst checking the route on the map and armed with the weather forecast expected for the day ahead, it was time to head off.

From the outset, I knew this would be a difficult day; however, in my mind, I accepted this and prepared myself for the day ahead, come what may.

The sheer pain experienced at the very start of the walk, having to cross grey/blue sharp stone chippings that formed the path to the bridge where the weir meets the vast Ennerdale Water would have made almost all "normal" people give up there and then. There was no escaping it either. The stone chippings were as far as the eye could see and trying to walk across them was bloody painful, so bad it brought on an instant sickly feeling with each step I took. It seemed to take forever to cross about 200 feet of this path and I wasn't prepared for this sudden inhospitable feeling under foot. In 13 months of training for this adventure challenge I thought I had covered most types of surfaces I would be walking on;

however, it appears this man-made terrain was overlooked in my training days.

After what felt like an eternity, I was off the harshness of the stone chippings and onto more of a manageable path with quick wins of grass here and there at the sides of it. I figured if the path was like this all the way round Ennerdale Water then I would have the day nailed and in the bag. It was too good to be true though and within half a mile of starting the day I encountered the worst trail ever, worse than the stone chippings and one that would see me push myself beyond any limits I thought I had.

The path went from rocky/grassy/stony to a brutal rock trail that appeared to be impossible to walk through and one that just wanted to carve my feet open and snap my ankles at every opportunity it could get. There was no grass, and I genuinely began to think this point on the route was impassable without hiking boots on.

Thankfully, my head works in a way that allows me to understand that in life hurdles present themselves to us all, that hurdles are there to challenge us and they can be overcome, and to me, this was now one of those times. I had two options, one, give it up as a bad job or two, figure it out.

In life, I believe we can figure everything out. Life isn't plain sailing at the best of times, but so many people simply give up when the going gets tough. I knew that finding a small positive in this current situation would help me figure out a plan to get me through this, no matter how long it took.

My key to cracking this deadlock between me and mother nature came in the form of a stream cutting across the rocks in front of me. I stood in this ice-cold crystal-clear running water while I was figuring out what to do and I noticed how the pain in my feet eased off considerably. I figured part of the problem was my feet had been traumatised when forced to walk through the stone chippings earlier and were throbbing and very sore. If I could reduce this pain and throbbing, then they will regain some of their use to help carry me over this awful patch of rock. I also knew that this rocky trail wouldn't last forever, and any severe pain would only be temporary. I cooled down my feet to a point where it was borderline that I could still feel them and decided this slight numbness would get me through to a point where I could dunk them in a puddle again further along this challenging part of the trail.

It was a great theory that worked albeit temporarily, but then the trail got even worse!

I was now in effect halfway through the rocky nightmare and sat thinking to myself, "I'm stuck". Two people were walking towards me on the trail and as they got closer, I realised it was Andy and his wife who I met yesterday. I played down the real situation I was in and said I was taking a breather for the benefit of my feet. What Andy didn't realise is I was stuck. Whether I went back on my tracks or carried on forward, I was literally stuck in a kind of hell.

I always imagined hell to look like some dark, fiery pit and not a place with spectacular views of a lake and mountains baked in sunshine like it was right now.

I got a grip of my thoughts and reminded myself that the pain is temporary and that each step I took was a step out of the grips of hell. With this determination I made my way through the rock and was pretty much through the roughest part of the path when Ian appeared. Having him around gave me an instant boost and his shoulder served as a great support for me to grab onto to help get me through the last few feet of sharp rock, seeing as I had forgotten my walking pole in my haste to get on with the start of my day.

13 months of training couldn't have prepared me for the paths around Ennerdale and they were so brutal under bare feet that it took 3 hours to travel 1 mile!

In my chat with Andy, he mentioned this was the hardest part of this trail around Ennerdale and apart from a bit of a technical scramble not too far ahead at Anglers Crag, the paths will get better. This was music to my ears. Andy was on his 5th crossing of the Coast to Coast and he knew the route very well so him telling me things would get better really picked me up.

A short distance from the pits of hell the path split into what appeared to be left and right trails. The right path involved a scramble, something I didn't fancy in bare feet and the left seemed friendlier so I took that as I believed it would take me on a lazy path around the crag face. This was Anglers Crag, the crag Andy was on about, yet I did not realise it, thinking it was just another challenging part of the trail so I should have taken the right path and accepted the scramble.

Nearing the point where the left path appeared to disappear off view, it suddenly gave way, and I plummeted down the rock face. My fall was broken by a 6-inch ledge of rock jutting out that my left foot came into contact with, stopping me dead in my tracks.

From my search and rescue training, I knew I had limited time before fear began to creep in which had the potential for me to make bad decisions. Given the extreme situation I was now in, I couldn't afford to make any bad decisions so had to take a deep breath, embrace the fear, think about this situation and do whatever I could to figure it out.

I used my body weight to push myself back into the rocky chasm I was now in ensuring I was as safe as I could be. My thoughts turned to my left foot and how long I could support my weight on it before tiredness crept in as this foot was the one thing keeping me from plummeting to the abyss below.

I also knew that facing outwards made it impossible for me to climb back up the side of the crag and if I wanted to get out of this situation, I had no option but to turn around and attempt to climb back up it.

The panic was now setting in at a rapid pace. I knew Ian was above me somewhere and that he would by now have noticed that I'd disappeared off the radar and wonder what was going on.

I started shouting for help as loud as I could. I knew there were other walkers on the trails above me so even if Ian had not realised I was down the side of the crag, others may hear my cries for help.

To me, my cries sounded silent. I was shouting as loud as I could; however, it seemed like the mountains and expanse of water in front of me were silencing my voice. I reached for the satellite tracker and began contemplating pressing the SOS button which would have triggered an emergency rescue and instantly end the barefoot adventure. "Was there an alternative", I thought to myself? "Can I get out of this situation without killing myself?".

I was now weighing up the dangers of this bad situation. It would take the emergency services some time to get to me I thought, so I figured trying shouting for help a few more times would give me a real chance to get off the side of the crag and allow me to continue with my challenge.

I really started to think to myself that my luck had finally run out on my adventure challenges and this could be the end. I also knew this was a great time for the demons to creep in and cloud my judgement and needed to fight them back as now wasn't the time.

After what felt like an eternity, I suddenly heard, "Don't move. I'm coming down for you". It was Ian. "Thank fuck!", I thought. If there's one person I knew could help me in this situation, it was Ian. We had served for many years in search and rescue and knew how each other worked in extreme situations, and this was one extreme situation to be in right now.

Having my backpack on with the weight of my kit in it had the chance to offset my balance, however it also had a loop on the back of it, giving Ian something to grab onto as I tried delicately to turn around on this 6-inch ledge.

My heart was beating out of my chest as I tried to turn around on this small piece of rock and swap my left foot for my right. I extended my right arm across my chest and tried to feel for anything that I could hold on to as I edged my way slowly around. My left arm was also behind me trying to feel for something to grip onto. I just hoped the weight in my backpack didn't tip me off balance as it would mean falling backwards and it was a long way down to the bottom.

Once I was facing the rock face, I looked around and felt for pieces of rock to grab on to that would take my weight. The rock face was smooth with limited gripping points, and on top of this, there were no footholds. Ian was using all his strength to drag me up the side of the crag and I needed to assist him with this wherever I could. I was praying the loop on the backpack would not snap whist being dragged up the face of the rock.

I was shouting to Ian to not let go of me and his reply was "I'm not letting go of you, you are not going anywhere". This one statement killed the fear in an instant and I found myself back in control and pulling myself up on anything I could get hold of until I reached the safety of the trail above me. Ian only released his grip on me when he knew I was safe.

I was now in a safe place and in true style, me and Ian had our obligatory man hug and patted each other reassuringly on the back and returned to the trail.

For most people, what happened over the last half an hour of me being rescued would have been sufficient for them to give up as it was a traumatic event.

Whilst it affected me, I thought to myself that I'm safe and other than skin coming off the tops of my feet because of having no footholds to climb back up the crag on and being dragged, I'm OK, so why let it stop the challenge from continuing? I knew if I thought about what had happened it would become the feeding ground for the demons to try to convince me to quit. It would lead to overthinking of the situation and have a negative impact on my mojo, so I locked it away and categorised it in my head as "an experience", allowing me to press on with the long day still ahead of me.

The weirdest part of this experience was I now felt more energised and raring to take on the day ahead of me than I was prior to falling down the side of the crag. I had taken a negative situation and used the power of it to create a positive mindset, rather than have it hang over me like a black cloud.

The trail got better as Andy had mentioned and soon Ennerdale was behind me and I was walking across green fields which felt amazing under foot.

The original plan was to head past YHA Ennerdale (High Gillerthwaite) and along the paths hugging the River Liza, ending up at YHA Black Sail. Whilst taking a break for a pot noodle and soaking my feet in the river, a few locals were out enjoying the sunshine and persuaded me that the easiest route for someone in bare feet would be to go back to where we had come from and head along the trails on the opposite side of the river.

You normally can't beat local knowledge and with the time now at 25 past 2 in the afternoon, having taken 5 and a half hours to cover 3 miles I felt that if things would be easier under foot, then I could claw back some losses that the rescue created and regular pit stops I had to take up till now due to the terrain. An average speed so far of half-a-mile per hour reflected the pure harshness of the Lakeland environment.

Heading through Ennerdale Forest proved to be just as slow under foot and whilst it was forest trail which should have been easier, it was very boggy in places and rocky in others. This meant my average mph varied from as low as 0.4mph and as high as 2mph depending where I was walking.

By now both Ian and I were low on water and if we didn't get to a main landmark on the route called Black Sail Hut soon, we would have no option but to divert to the river and take water from there. It would mean an impact on time because the water would have to be boiled off and cooled down before we could drink it to ensure any nasties were obliterated, otherwise we risked bad belly symptoms and being in the middle of nowhere, this wouldn't be fun.

The evening sun was beating down and making the mountains surrounding us look golden and warm. Where we were right now was the best place in the world to be. It was so remote, and it made me feel a million miles away from town life and all the hustle and bustle pace that goes with it. I felt at one with nature and its beautiful surroundings.

It took 4 and a quarter hour to get from the end of Ennerdale Water where the locals gave me their advice on which trail to take to get to Black Sail Hut, completing 4 and a half miles, meaning my average speed was a little over 1mph. I had to question if it would have been any quicker had I not listened to the local advice? It was after all the same distance, just a different terrain. It's something I'll never know unless I go back and try it barefoot.

Black Sail Hut is a very remote retreat for hikers, and the only way to get to it is on foot or by mountain bike. It is situated right on the Coast to Coast route and is often used by travellers wanting to break up their crossing of the country and explore the nearby peaks such as Red Pike and Great Gable.

Arriving at the hut, I walked in and the first thing I did was make a beeline for the kitchen to grab some water. I was so thirsty, having ran out of the ration of water that I had in my bottle a mile back down the path, so grabbed a pint glass and filled it up with ice cold water and drank it down in 1 go. It felt amazing, ice cold and wet, so amazing in fact I did it again! I know I should have been sipping the water and not gulping it down, but I didn't care. I had a dehydrated headache and fluid was the key to getting rid of it.

Being the only ones at Black Sail, the lady managing the hut allowed us full use of the facilities, drink pints of water and refill our water bottles. After chilling out in the main room on a bench for a short while to rest my feet and allow my body to feel better than it had been feeling throughout the day, it was soon time to get ready to press on once again. I knew it was time to move on as I had got the onset of the shivers and this is a sign to me that my body wants to shut itself off for the rest of the day.

Given it was only 7.30pm and after a study of the OS map, we decided to press on to Honister before nightfall. Ideally the end point for the day would have been Rosthwaite, but taking into consideration the very slow going at the start of the day because of the terrible terrain, and the rescue from the side of the mountain, this was now out of reach given there was still 4 and a half miles to go to get to Rosthwaite, involving hiking up mountains with only about 3 hours of useable daylight to get there.

Getting to Honister still involved hiking further into the mountains; however, compared to Rosthwaite, it was only a couple of miles away as the crow flies and achievable. It needed to be achievable as there was no middle point to jump off at should we need to. Honister was literally the next main place with a road and nothing but mountains in the way so the motivation was to get there or end up having to spend a night on the mountain which I didn't fancy doing.

Leaving the safety of Black Sail Hut behind, ahead was a steep climb out of the valley via Seavy Knot. This involved ascending and scrambling over rocks and boulders on the side of a deep scar that allowed Loft Beck to flow through it, which was challenging enough in hiking boots let alone bare feet. It took 45 minutes to ascend the 600 feet or so to reach the top of the mountain and the views that unfolded were spectacular. The sun was behind us as I reached the top and I saw Ian making some weird gestures to himself. What the hell was he doing? Had he lost the plot? He can't have altitude sickness as the point I was standing on by now was only 1,700ft above sea level.

It turned out he was making shadow puppets at the top of the mountain in the dying sunshine of the day and I have to be honest; he was doing a cracking job at it.

Thankfully, it was pretty flat once on the tops, accompanied with an abundance of grassy trail, meaning for the remaining one and a half miles I could up my average speed. I was cruising along at a nice 1.8mph however what happened next wasn't planned, nor was it experienced at any point in my training.

Pushing on into the evening, one thing that has always amazed me is how rapidly you lose the light in the Lake District when the sun goes down over the mountains. Temperatures can suddenly plummet and carrying extra layers to mitigate the chances of becoming hypothermic is a must. Hypothermia is a potentially dangerous situation when body temperature drops rapidly, often caused by a prolonged exposure to cold temperatures. This is always a risk factor when in the hills at any time of the year, and one every hiker should know.

Walking barefoot across the tops of the mountains put me in a situation I hadn't even thought about. I had the extra layers and was now wearing them as the temperature had dropped significantly, however I was also walking ankle deep in water because of the heavy rains experienced in this part of the country recently, leaving the high ground sodden. It wasn't long before I started losing the feeling in my feet. Was this frostbite setting in? The rest of my body was warm; however, my feet began to feel like blocks of ice. With some distance still to cover and the light fading fast, it was now imperative I got off this mountain.

The light was completely lost by 10.30pm, and luckily this only affected the final descent into Honister Slate Mine.

After the day I had been through, it was great to see my support team and be able to tuck into a massive bowl of pasta Bolognese and diced ham.

What a day it's been, 3 hours to do one mile because of the sheer harshness of the terrain, having to be rescued off the side of a mountain, a water emergency and then frostbite. The demons will have a field day tonight trying to convince me to quit and they were already beginning to rear their heads and chip away at me.

Feeling cold, having very sore feet and a belly full of food, I was beat and ready to crawl into my sleeping bag. It wasn't long before I passed out with the tiredness ravaging my body.

Day 3

Honister Slate Mine

to Grasmere

After a late finish yesterday, attempting to claw back some lost time from my rescue off the side of the mountain at Ennerdale, I woke up to a spectacular sunny morning in the valley at Seathwaite, surrounded by mountains and no mobile phone signal. If ever I wanted to get away from it all and become isolated from my fast-paced life, this was it.

The mountain sides were basking in a golden blanket of light and the sky was a true-blue colour with not a cloud anywhere to be seen. In the Lake District it's bad weather or good; there's never any in between in this part of the world. Today it was better than good.

Overnight the skin on my feet had gone very taught, and it felt like I could no longer bend them. This wasn't a good start. My feet were a mess from yesterday's injuries caused primarily from my ass being rescued from the side of the mountain. Having no foot holds and being dragged up the rocky face of the mountain, the skin on the tops of my feet bore the brunt of it. For 15 miles, the terrain had been so brutal it had caused holes to appear in the sole of my left foot, causing nauseating pain. There was no blood, just 2 deep gaping holes in the sole of my foot.

I needed to pee and with each step I took, the taught skin on my feet split open like it was tissue paper. The pain level was the worst I have ever experienced causing a sickly feeling to come over me.

I had major barefoot miles ahead of me through the mountains and I was finding it difficult to just walk across a field to take a piss. "This is going to be a tough day," I thought to myself.

If this was the outcome for my feet after just 2 barefoot days on the Coast to Coast, what will they be like after 2 weeks? Will I cause permanent damage to my feet? Should I give up?

The little dark demons were coming out and taking over my thoughts, whispering a million excuses to me about why I should quit, even using the lovely morning in the mountains as an excuse to sack it all in and just chill out for the day.

The caffeine kick from a strong cup of coffee really woke me up and with that I had to figure out how to get my feet working to take on the day ahead.

Given the skin on the tops of my feet was now split open and having wandered off for a piss, it allowed more flexibility to bend them. I found that by rocking them heels to balls (of feet) it helped get the blood flowing in my feet again and eased them up. It was painful but allowed my feet to behave in a way that normal feet worked.

I applied some manuka honey foot cream to my feet and after initially stinging the open wounds; I found it beginning to help make the skin more subtle, helping my feet to move easier. I tried to apply some liquid skin to the open wounds to help protect them from the nasties ahead, but on application the stinging sensation was so intense it brought tears to my eyes. Boy, it stung!

"Sod that" I thought. I had Savlon with me so applied that gently to the wounds on my feet and allowed it to seep in whilst I finished my coffee.

I needed to come up with a daily morning foot ritual if this was how things would be, to ensure my feet worked for the day ahead. There was absolutely no way I could get up and just go out there into the mountains for the day without bringing my feet back to life from overnight rest.

Hobbling around getting my gear ready for the day ahead was painful, but it allowed my feet to exercise.

Soon it was time to leave this idyllic little place in the valley behind me and pick up where I left off in the dark last night. The demons in my head telling me to quit didn't win today.

It was time to let the world know I was on my way for day 3 so I switched on the satellite tracker and let it lock onto the satellite network before I set off. The good thing with the satellite tracker is it doesn't need 4G phone signal to communicate with the outside world and instead uses the global network of satellites orbiting around us all to ensure my location is continually tracked. The safety aspect of this is if I was in a spot of bother and there was no 4G signal to place an emergency call, just like this moment in time being right in the thick of the mountains and having no 4G on my phone, I had a big red button saying SOS on the tracker and if pressed; it got through to a rescue centre regardless of my location. All big brother stuff I know, but the safety aspect is immeasurable.

I had hoped to have made it to Rosthwaite by the end of the day yesterday, however the rescue set this back and given I had completely lost the light last night, it left me 2 and a half kilometres short of my end point for the day, meaning I had the distance to do on top of today's mileage.

It was a good call though, because coming off the road and onto the trail that would lead me into Rosthwaite would have been dangerous to try to complete in the dark with just a head torch on. The trail was littered with scree, dolomite and stone, and the grass verges that would give me the "quick wins" were often only a foot wide at some points with a steep drop off to the right. I'm sure you will agree, all very dangerous in the dark when my next step could have been off the side of the mountain.

From the off, the going was slow because of the very challenging terrain and every step I took seemed to resonate pain that was felt throughout my body, even pulsing in my temples.

Being a Monday morning, I wasn't expecting it to be too busy on the trails, thus allowing me to plod along uninterrupted at my paltry average speed of 1.5mph, however,

I was quite surprised to see quite a few people out enjoying the fells. This meant I was being stopped here and there by people being inquisitive as to what I was doing. I wasn't bothered in the slightest as it meant I could stop for a few minutes and take the pressure off my feet while I was talking to them.

Eventually I was passing the trail next to Johnny Wood and having been down here in the past I knew there was a fiddly bit to cross involving a rope and rock. This would be interesting in bare feet as I remember it being challenging enough in hiking boots when I passed across this point a few years ago.

Ian was with me and stood in the stream, poised with the film camera, just in case I fell on my ass at this point as I edged my way round the slippy rocks, holding on to the rope with one hand and using my walking pole in the other hand to create some kind of stability, given my feet don't have the same grip as hiking boots.

After 10 minutes of navigating a distance of 200 feet around this tricky part of the trail, I was off again and closing in on YHA Borrowdale. Normally I would just press on past a YHA building, however given that I was low on calories and had some excruciating pain going on in my feet, stopping was a necessity and the YHA building on my route was a real blessing.

Ian offered to buy the coffee and cake whilst I sorted the seat outside for us and tended to my feet.

Sitting outside with my crazy hat on and bare feet brought a few stares from groups of people passing through the trail. One nice older gentleman asked me if I was OK and should he call for medical help? Bless him.

I assured him all was fine, and that I was merely taking a much-needed break from my barefoot Coast to Coast Walk. "Your barefoot what? Are you for real?" was the reply, a reaction I have become accustomed to since I set off on this adventure 2 and a half days ago.

Orange cake and caffeine tasted so nice and the sugar gave me a real kick... or was it the caffeine?

Given it was now just after midday I needed to get a wiggle on and get moving as there was still a shit load of miles to do for the day ahead. Whilst Ian got his gear together, I took our water bottles and topped them up to the max from the communal water bottle filling stations as we would not be seeing any support until the end of the day, so we had to be self-sufficient. Water is the most important thing to carry on any adventure, however it's heavy and bulky to carry in quantity so judging the right amount for the journey ahead is very important. The downside is this journey is unpredictable in how long it will take to get to an endpoint as the terrain dictates the speed for me, and I was in the middle of the mountains and on trails that are complicated enough even with appropriate footwear on.

Crossing over and intercepting the trail at Stonethwaite, the path became noticeably more difficult to walk on, bringing my average speed down in places to less than a mile an hour. The "quick wins" of grass verges were nowhere to be seen and ahead of me was just awash with stones, boulders and scree.

I began crossing a difficult part of the path which was covered in stones and boulders, and I was struggling in a big way as each step I took had the potential to either break an ankle or slice a foot open. Whilst I had my head down concentrating on each step and using my pole to balance myself, I heard a voice bellow "Get out of the way!". I looked up to find a group of older retirees displeased that I was holding them up.

Ian explained what I was doing, however they had no interest and just wanted to be past me and began forcing me out of the way and barging past, one by one. So Rude!!! In fact, so rude, they got a dedication in the front of this book! Impatient Arseholes!

They could see how I was struggling to walk across these boulders and the scree, but it mattered not to them if I bust an ankle or sustained another injury, just as long as they got past.

Soon the "older ones" were a distant memory, and I was heading up the mountain and passing the spectacular views of Eagle Crag to the right of me. The trail was a lot kinder on my feet with grassy areas in abundance. Looking back down the valley from where I had come from earlier, I couldn't believe that I had made it this far through the Lake District with no shoes and socks on.

Continuing my ascent up the trails and onto the tops at Grasmere Common, I was faced with what looked like an impossible scramble up and over Lining Crag. This looked like a very steep and technical scramble and it worried me that one wrong foot out of place here would create great injury. There was no real way around this as I needed to be up and over this crag and to make things a little more difficult, it began to rain.

That did it, I couldn't hang around any longer contemplating going up and over the crag, I just had to do it as the rain would make it even more difficult to get a grip on things with my bare feet if I didn't get on with it.

Being barefoot and faced with a steep rocky crag to scramble over isn't a good combination especially in the rain but "it is what it is" and I had to get this done. Ian scouted out the best way he could find for me that would be a safe route on a difficult and technical crag. This guy just had my back in situations like this. He knew I wasn't feeling confident about this scramble, especially after the situation I found myself in yesterday, however he did everything he could to help put my mind at ease. Ultimately though, it was me who had to do this, and I was now beginning to battle the demons telling me to quit, trying to convince me it was too tough and very dangerous.

In life, I am a believer that I can figure everything out, no matter what situation I face. To me, this was just another one of those times. I turned the demons around and used my fear as a springboard to ensure I got across the crag and over the other side safely.

Fear is the inbuilt safety mechanism in us all that will ultimately help us in a situation or frighten us off. I like to think of fear as False Evidence Appearing Real whereby you can Face Everything And Rise above the situation, as opposed to Fuck Everything And Run from the situation.

My ass was nipping as I made it to the top of this steep crag, however the feeling of accomplishment was fantastic once over the top of it. I had conquered a steep technical crag, a crag challenging enough for anyone in boots, in my bare feet and in the rain. I definitely Faced Everything my demons were hitting me with And Rose above them. Suggs 1, Demons 0... again.

Once on the other side of the crag it was time for a breather and a man hug with Ian to say thanks for his scouting out of the best way he could find for me to get this safely in the bag. After a breather and a much-needed rest of my feet, letting the rain cool them down, the crossing of Grasmere Common began.

Walking across the top of the mountain range seemed to go on forever, and the rain ensured the ground was very boggy and wet, cooling and soothing my sore feet and once again making them look all wrinkly like they had been in a bath for hours.

After an hour of walking across the Common, the rain passed, and the sun was back out and shining in the valleys ahead, lifting the temperature with it.

Descending off the tops of the mountain seemed to last forever with so many false mountain end points, hoping this was the last one to go down, before realising it goes down again to another level, and another before a long lazy final descent into Grasmere itself.

The last stretch into civilisation was through a forest and I have to say, this path was the worst I had encountered throughout the whole day. My average mph wasn't even hitting half a mile an hour at this point. I was cold, tired, sore and the best way to describe the final hundred steps of the day was pure, painful torture.

I had been at this for 11 hours and truthfully; I was feeling quite broken.

Alone with my thoughts this evening, I felt low, very low. My eyes were filling up all the time, crying but not crying, on an emotional edge and I didn't know why. This was only the end of day 3 and I wasn't even halfway through the Lake District yet. I needed to get a grip and sort myself out.

The pain in my now openly bleeding feet was so bad it was preventing me from sleeping. I suppose it is like toothache in a way. The more you think about it, the worse it seems, especially in the dead of night.

The rain had returned, and it was bouncing down, lasting all night. I love the sound of rain and find it therapeutic to sleep to, however given the pain from my feet keeping me awake, this just added to not being able to sleep.

Day 4

Grasmere to Patterdale

Having had 3 hours sleep overnight, I was absolutely shattered! Even my daily morning meditation session sent me back off into a broken sleep.

The day began once again by exercising my feet and splitting the taught skin to allow some freedom of movement. Rocking my feet heels to balls made the skin on my feet crack open in front of my eyes. There was literally nothing I could do about this as I needed my feet working so I had to suck it up.

Lack of mobility in my feet is a hard feeling to describe, however, the throbbing pain and open sores were literally making me feel sick.

One thing that wasn't impacted with this pain level was my motivation. So far on the adventure, and no matter the state of my feet, the lack of sleep or the bad weather, I knew the day needed tackling, and I was eager to get on with it. I just needed to build in the feet exercises first to every future day of the adventure.

Today's plan was to head back into the mountains and cross over to Patterdale and whilst this would be one of the shortest legs of the whole journey, being only 7 miles as the crow flies, it involved navigating a lot of difficulties in the mountains and other challenging terrain.

Prior to setting off, the weather began to turn again, and the grey overcast start of the morning so far was now being replaced with rain and wind.

"4 days in, I should be used to this by now," I thought to myself.

The time to head off was now upon me, so the tracker was switched on, a final gear check was conducted, and I was off.

Hobbling across a stony area of road to a big patch of grass I was making tracks and soon passing Thorny How and following the road up to Mill Bridge. The road surface wasn't too bad under foot, allowing me to walk at an impressive 1.8mph. The rain was also acting as a cooling agent for the tops of my feet, with the wet road surface cooling the soles.

Simple little things like this were having a very positive effect on my mind and feet.

Crossing the A591 I was soon back on challenging terrain, reducing my average walking speed vastly. The ground was now a mix of stone, dolomite and rock and the "quick wins" of grass to ease the impact and pain on my feet were in short supply, plus I was ascending the side of a fell.

Eventually I faced a ford which once crossed led to the start of Little Tongue, my route onto the tops of the fell.

It was windy as hell and holding my walking pole out by the hand loop saw the power of the wind lift it into a horizontal position. The wind ripped your breath out of your lungs when having to deal with it face on.

Thankfully, the sun had now made an appearance, however after the amount of rain dumped on the area of late, the ground was soaking wet and could not absorb the sheer amount of water on it. Combined with a steep climb in a strong head wind, I made it to the top, or at least I thought it was the top, till I realised it was a false summit and there was still a good way to go to get to the "real" top of the mountain and onto Hause Riggs.

It was here that the terrain became an absolute bitch as I made my way up to Hause Gap on Grisedale Hause. The paths were carved into the terrain and scree was as far as the eye could see. "This would be slow to get through, but totally do-able", I thought to myself. It had to be do-able as the only way off this mountain if it wasn't was by helicopter.

The going was tough and slow, and I figured it was time for a pot noodle break with Ian, using the time to rest my feet and re-align my focus to get me through this challenging segment of the route.

Approaching the gap that would take us down to Grisedale Tarn it once again rained. The cloud began descending on us and the wind was now whipping up waterspouts on Grisedale Tarn below us.

Heading down the path at the side of Grisedale Tarn, the rain was now battering us, and it felt like the wind was driving needles into my face. I pulled my hood tighter over my head to a position where only my eyes were exposed to the weather. Ian was ahead of me and struggling to batten down his own hatches and minimise the effect the weather was having on him.

On the opposite side of Grisedale Tarn I could see people making a hasty descent off Dollywagon Pike. I thought to myself "The weather isn't nice this side of the tarn at this height, so god only knows what the hikers higher up on Dollywagon Pike were experiencing with the weather. Rather them though and not me,".

Heading down the side of Tarn, Falcon and Sprout Crags was literally stop/start. The trails were once again made up of pure scree and I found myself at one point using my arse to drag myself through a treacherous section by sitting down and using my hands to lift me up, shuffle past the evil bits and drop it back down. It was absolute hell once again getting through this almost impassable by bare feet place.

Once released from these jaws of hell and heading into the valley, the temperature dropped considerably because of the inclement weather and I reached for the extra layers to keep my body warm. My feet were already numb from the pain so this change in temperature didn't seem to bother them like it had done on previous days.

The scree of the crags was now behind me and an abundance of grass opened up ahead of me. It was wet and very waterlogged, but still, it was grass and not scree!

Continuing down the trail from Grisedale Forest I came across Ruthwaite Lodge Climbing Hut. Ruthwaite Lodge is a well-built and maintained stone building that faces out into the valley below. This was an ideal place to take a pit stop after some rough going on the descent so far.

After a rest and a bit of banter with Ian, I continued down the track which was filling up with people all descending into Patterdale as part of their Coast to Coast journey. Rather than slow these folks down with my paltry pace on the rocky path, I made use of the grassy side of the valley and descend that way.

With the valley being steep, my walk turned into a run which got faster as I descended further. Despite having sore feet, I was in complete control of this run as this was probably the best surface I had experienced throughout the adventure so far.

In the distance below, I could see a footbridge which was presenting the option of a left or right path to take on either side of it. Having left Ian way behind up the side of the valley, I kept running to the bridge, took a breather there and waited for him.

Nearing the bridge there was a group of students and two mountain leaders all sat around chilling out, and as I ran past them, they all got up and cheered and clapped me past. What a boost they gave me.

Despite my feet giving me pain, I felt great! I felt like I was doing an Olympic sprint down the side of the valley, when in reality I didn't even cross 4mph. Considering my average pace throughout the adventure so far was 1.5mph, this was a super-fast pace to achieve.

Whilst chilling at the foot bridge waiting for Ian to descend, I began chatting with people who too were waiting for others in their parties to come down the path from the mountain. The bridge became our communal waiting place. Chat alternated between my feet, my hat, which path to take, how people have found it so far and so on. The consensus from everyone was to take the right-hand side path when you look down the valley.

Following the right-hand path down the valley, the world began to flatten out more. The terrain was still tough under foot in places; however, it was also balanced with grassy "quick wins".

The final stretch was now only a mile and a half away, yet when this distance was covered under bare foot, it seemed like it was 5 miles.

Popping out onto the main road at Grisedale Bridge, I headed right en route to the end point of the day at YHA Patterdale, some half a mile up the road. Whilst I was making my way slowly on the paths, Ian went ahead to catch the support team for some water.

The paths in Patterdale are first rate if you have appropriate footwear on, however in bare feet it translated into some aggressively coated tarmac type paths, creating a great grip for hiking boot soles, however a nightmare for bare skin soles to walk on.

I dropped onto the road where it was smoother and walked towards the oncoming traffic on the white line at the side edge of the road. Walking or running towards the oncoming traffic is the safe and adopted way to do things under foot as you can see the oncoming traffic and can take swift action in a dangerous situation, and they can see you a lot better as well.

Painted white lines on a road surface are smooth and are absolutely heaven to walk on with no shoes and socks on.

Walking on the white lines, I was feeling pretty broken after the transit through the mountains and had my head down, feeling like a very weary traveller.

Looking up to check for traffic, I saw a policeman ahead of me who had by now firmly locked his gaze onto me. "You aren't going to nick me for walking on white lines, are you?" I said to him as I got within conversation distance. He started laughing, assured me I wasn't getting nicked and asked me what it was all about. I'm sure a guy in a crazy multicoloured hat and bare feet isn't a regular sight in Patterdale.

I explained my adventure and the charitable causes I was doing it for, and the policeman shook my hand, wished me all the best and got on with doing his Policing duties.

Continuing my walk along the white line, a Canadian tourist ran out of one of the hotels on the roadside and yelled "Not only is the crazy barefoot guy in town.... but so is the Royal Family... LOOK!".

A bit bewildered and surprised with his comments, I turned around and sure enough, coming down the side of the hill opposite, amongst tight security was William and Kate.

In no time at all, they were off the mountain and visited Deepdale Hall Farm just opposite where we were.

In the distance there was a thunderous noise building up, and popping out of the low cloud a helicopter descended into the valley, landing in Ullswater, before eventually heading off with its royal passengers aboard. By now a crowd of us were stood watching as the helicopter hovered in the distance, turned and disappeared into the low valley mist that was now descending ever closer to the ground.

It's a shame William and Kate never had time to meet "The Barefoot Crazy Hat Man". I'm sure it would have made their day and inspired them both, ha!

By the time I arrived at YHA Patterdale it was 4.30pm and this was an early finish compared to previous days, but a welcomed one as my feet were so sore and bleeding again.

Running down the side of the valley earlier seemed very therapeutic for my feet, although I suspect it will definitely impact them in the days ahead. My energy levels were low, and my mind was darkening again. It's as if the demons knew I had now finished the day so tried to befriend my head and feed me every excuse to quit this madness.

My focus was soon diverted to my hands. The weather in the mountains had been so extreme today that the skin on my fingers had split open, leaving deep open caverns that strangely never bled but were suddenly feeling sore.

Truthfully, I was so glad to be back in civilisation and off the mountains.

Despite trying to hold the demons at bay, my mind was feeling like it was entering a bit of a dark place.

I love the Lake District; however, right now I just want out of it. I'm 4 days in with a lot of very challenging days still ahead of me.

I knew from the outset that the most challenging part of this adventure would be in the Lake District National Park with its major mountains and challenging terrain. I also factored in bad weather during the planning stages of the adventure challenge, however, the weather experienced today was bloody horrendous, far worse than I could have imagined it to be at any stage of the planning. There's nothing that could be done about it either as in the mountains, you are exposed to whatever weather is thrown at you, leaving you feeling almost trapped in your surroundings, and you only have the kit that you take with you in your backpack to help you out of the situation, or at least make it more manageable.

The dark mists were now clouding my head with all the negative things, the pain in my feet, the lack of skin on my feet, the weather, and now my fingers and I was finding it hard to wade through these negatives and flip to the positives that happened throughout the day.

Normally this isn't a problem, however extreme challenges sometimes make it difficult to easily grasp at the positive things that happen. Extreme adventure situations aren't normal, and everything is magnified, both good and bad, way bigger than they are in reality.

I wanted to talk to Ian about the way I was feeling but I couldn't open up. I'm supposed to be superhuman to these guys and feel I will be letting my guard down if I was to let on my true feelings about how I am feeling after just 4 days.

It was a struggle just to get my head into the map tonight and plan tomorrows segment that would see me take on 15 miles of barefoot walking through the last remaining part of the Lake District.

And there it was!! My motivational hook to kick the demons out and let the positivity flood through was there, right in front of me. Tomorrow would be my last day in the Lake District and the world would get flatter after this. This was so positive! I noticed tonight was also the first glint of things beginning to impact Ian. He was quiet, not a tired quiet, just a quiet one sentence type of guy. He needed his space to figure things out too, and I respected that.

54

Day 5

Patterdale to Shap

After around 4 hours sleep because of the constant rain, and the strong throbbing pains in my feet, I was awake and fumbling around for my phone to get my guru music on so I could meditate and frame my mind for the day ahead.

Ahead of me today was 14 and a half hours of barefoot walking and what would be the last push out of the Lake District, one that would take me back into the mountains before descending and flattening out a bit as I made my way to my end point of Shap.

No matter what the world threw at me today, I was turning up in Shap. It was non-negotiable.

I now wanted to be out of the harshness of the Lake District and hitting Shap signified this to me. I set the goal in my head. Shap at all costs, no matter the time of day or night I got there.

I love the Lake District and all its splendour, having adventured here since being a young lad, but, on this adventure, I just want it out of the way and behind me as the last few days have been tough, and truthfully not enjoyable in the slightest.

My morning ritual of feet exercises to split the taught skin open was soon complete, and I went from a hobble, to someone who looked like they had half a clue how to walk.

The weather wasn't the best AGAIN, and I knew I had a tough day ahead of me as my feet were now coming up to five days into this adventure and suffering with the pain, even when not in contact with the ground. When meditating I had set my end goal solid in my head, saw my end goal, felt it was real and now all I had to do was make it happen.

Positive visualisation has helped me achieve so much success in life, be it adventuring, private life and in my working life.

To positively visualise a successful end result, I take myself into a relaxed place, see the end goal as it has actually happened. I notice the faces around me, my views of the place I am at, for instance, today's end place of Shap, I visualise the buildings, the smells, any touch points; all enforcing the positive end goal has happened and was a success. It embeds the goal in my head, ensuring I complete it.

The only reality then is to fill in all the blanks in real time to get to the end goal and figure out any stumbling blocks that get in the way.

As I have previously mentioned in other chapters in this book, a major key to success is believing that anything can be figured out.

We constantly face setbacks in our daily lives and for most people, a hurdle, a stumbling block or whatever you want to call it is enough for them to throw the towel in and give up, bail out and call it a day. By not allowing defeat to come into a situation you can find ways around anything and figure out a new outcome for yourself and the circumstances you are in. Trust in yourself, accept things can go wonky from time to time and that they CAN be fixed.

Leaving the YHA at Patterdale and walking down the road to the bridge that crosses Goldrill Beck, it was soon time to start the ascent into the mountains again via the path up Stonebarrow Gill. Leaving the road and onto the path there was a vast change in terrain under foot. The path comprised sharp stone and signified a typical walkers trail. Luckily there were a good few "quick win" grassy edges to walk on as I headed further up to the top of the path. My speed was fluctuating between a top speed of 1.2mph on the quick grassy wins, and half a mile an hour on the challenging bits with no grassy areas.

Halfway up Stonebarrow Gill, the wind was picking up, and the cloud was steadily descending. Just another day in paradise, I thought to myself. And "It is what it is."

Ian had made tracks ahead of me as my speed admittedly was slow going. He was popping in and out of view with the low cloud now starting to eat up the visibility. Being an experienced man of the mountains like myself, Ian knew to take a pit stop and wait for me to get to him. Becoming detached and fragmented from your group in the fog is not safe at all.

Enveloped in the low cloud gave a very eerie feeling on the fell. Visibility was only 20 feet and other than the noise from Ian's hiking boots on the path, it was silent. Now and then the low cloud broke and visibility became a hundred feet or so and you could see the next batch of cloud heading towards you at a rate of knots as the wind drove it into the mountains.

My feet, once again, were becoming so cold it felt like frostbite was setting in. The paths were wet and harboured big unavoidable puddles that I had to walk through, and the grass was so wet that standing on it resulted in my feet sinking as the weight of me forced the water out of the ground.

Whilst the numbing feeling in my feet was masking the pain, I also knew this wasn't a good thing, especially as today was a 15 miler and I still had a good 11 hours ahead of me so I needed my feet to work, albeit in their diminished capacity.

That was it, I needed to warm them up, so turning my back into the wind to act as a windbreak I had no option but to piss on my feet. It sounds gross, but it had an immediate warming effect that took away the numbness for a short while.

I accepted the fact that as long as I was this high in the mountains in this atrocious weather, my feet would experience this level of cold, and the positive anchor I made in my head to help me push through this difficult time was "what goes up must eventually come down", where my feet would start warming up again and let the pain take over the numbness once again.

Passing Angle Tarn, the weather was raging and a torrent of rain and wind battering us. Angle Tarn on a good day has spectacular views attached to it, however walking the trail above it today was one of the worst places to be in the world.

By the time we had reached one of the highest points on the route at 696 metres (2,283ft) called Rest Dodd, it was near impossible to walk. Not just because of my feet; the wind was hitting me face on at a vast speed and driving the rain into my face, feet and hands like knives were being blown directly at me through an industrial fan.

There was no visibility around us at all and we had to do a map check to ensure we were on the right path and heading the right way.

Many a hiker has been caught out in situations like this where disorientation causes panic which leads to bad decision making and often resulting in Mountain Rescue and other emergency services being scrambled to help. The key here was to establish a known landmark and find it on the map, however with no visibility the use of a paper map was out of the question. Thankfully, in the mountains both me and Ian carry handheld GPS devices. Given the extreme weather we worked out of Ian's first and then fall back onto mine as a backup. Both devices had the route uploaded to them and with the aid of satellite positioning it showed us our exact position on the map despite having no visibility other than a radius of about 10 feet around us.

GPS devices are great for navigating but should never be a complete solution to be relied on as batteries can go dead. A paper map is essential for all trips in the mountains as a fallback. For this situation though, the paper map couldn't really help, and the digital mapping really came into its own.

Sitting down with our backs to the wind created a temporary reprieve from the wild weather and upon standing back up, I was almost blown over; that's how strong the wind was. I held the hand strap of my walking pole and allowed the wind to blow at it with its full force, resulting in the walking pole becoming horizontal and staying in that position, that was the sheer ferocity of the wind bearing down on us.

This had now become the most extreme weather I had faced in the Lake District EVER! And I have been in the mountains in the snow which wasn't as punishing as this. I needed to be off the tops of these mountains...and as quickly as possible.

After passing The Knott at 739 metres, we were soon at the highest point so far today, and the highest point we would get to for the rest of the day, Kidsty Pike at 780 metres (2,559 feet). In fact, this would be the highest point experienced for the rest of the adventure challenge, beyond this the mountains and hills would all be a lower height.

By now other hikers appeared out of the cloud and then disappearing straight back into it as they passed us, all looking very beat up by the weather. We met Rob Prance once again as he popped out of the cloud and he told us how he ended up getting disorientated because of the lack of visibility and began following what he thought was the right path. He ended up descending the valley and had to come back up. That's how quickly you can get lost in extreme situations like this.

Rob bade us farewell once again and disappeared off into the low cloud, as the speed I was walking wasn't the best because of the expanse of scree and rock scattered everywhere, and the low visibility made me scrutinise the ground more to make sure I was finding a safe path through the shitty bits.

Heading towards Kidsty Howes and the descent to Haweswater, Ian spotted 2 hikers backpacks over some rocky formations and near to the edge of a known steep drop. My first thought was "oh shit!" as you couldn't see much at all because of the extreme weather, and if two hikers had got themselves in difficulty, then it would be very hard to locate them. Approaching the backpacks, two heads rose from the rocky area and said "hi." The owners of the backpacks were taking refuge behind some rocks as they had been battered with the weather so much and needed an escape. "There were far better (and safer) places to get a reprieve from the weather than this place," I thought to myself.

Descending the side of the mountain into Haweswater took a lot of effort and time because of the terrain underfoot, an hour in fact, for what was a distance of half a kilometre. It was a descent in height of around 800ft.

Walking even a hundred feet down the mountain brought us under the weather system that had been battering the hell out of us all day, and as soon as we could see a horizon, the water, and even life below us, it lifted the spirits. Civilisation was back in our grasps.

Now was a perfect place to have a pit stop and eat a pot noodle. Whilst eating I could see Wood Howe, a small island on Haweswater and I began thinking to myself how cool it would be to live on it for a month as a future challenge. With the next mouthful of noodles, I told myself to get this adventure challenge in the bag first, before contemplating any other adventure.

The temperature shift at this point was also very dramatic. By coming under the weather system that had us in a constant cold grip for the past 7 hours, it was now feeling warmer, instantly bringing with it a great mental boost and the feeling back to my feet.

It was 3.20pm by the time I made it down the side of the mountain and through the gate to begin the walk around the edge of Haweswater. I was hoping this trail was not as bad as the one experienced on day 2 when I walked around Ennerdale Water.

Before starting along the path, a quick pit stop was in order to check the map and figure out how far it was to Shap. The map showed there was 6 miles still to go, meaning I had to average 1mph the rest of the way to get to Shap at a respectable time of night and still provide me with a bit of light to see where I was walking.

Heading off along the path the terrain was fairly manageable... very painful on my feet but manageable, despite there not being a lot of grassy quick wins to walk on. I have been to Haweswater many times in my life; however, I have never appreciated the sheer length of the water till now when I had to walk one side of it in bare feet. 3 miles long in fact, taking me over 4 hours to walk it. The path on the map looks level with the water itself, however, the reality is there was quite a bit of up and down to go with it which brought me under my 1mph average speed I needed to maintain.

After 4 hours of walking, I reached the other end of Haweswater and the trail went into a forest, before bringing me out at a place called Burnbanks. A very nice older gentleman stopped in his tracks when he saw me emerge from the wooded area, asked what I was doing, donated a fiver to the charity and even offered me and Ian a lift to Shap, which I declined and his expression was of the "is he mad?" kind of look. "It's raining, and this guy has no shoes and socks on, and he's refused a lift!!" I wonder what he thought about my crazy hat as well. Whatever he thought, he never asked about it or even attempted to.

Dan from my support team had been tracking my progress on the satellite tracker and was waiting for us near the phone box at Burnbanks with naughty calorie loaded pasties and bottles of water. This was the first time we had seen any of the support team for 11 hours as there was literally no place for them to intercept us on the route. Surprisingly, the water I took with me at the start of the day had only just ran out prior to seeing Dan. I guess the cold and shitty weather kept my body temperature down and reduced my need to want to drink as often as I normally do.

The rain was getting heavy once again so after a 10-minute pit stop for the naughty food; it was time to bid Dan farewell and head off down the path at Naddle Gate.

This path signified we were now well and truly out of the mountains and onto friendlier and more grassy terrain... AND only 3 miles away from Shap! Fantastic!

3 miles doesn't sound much of a distance, but barefoot and terrain dependent, that equates on average to another 3 hours of painful walking at 1mph. Given it was now half past 6 in the evening I estimated getting to Shap by half past 9 and still having a bit of light left for safety should I hit some challenging terrain on the way that had the potential to slow me down.

I found strength in knowing that the end point of the day was now within touching distance and despite it taking another 3 hours to get there; I ended up in Shap at 9.40pm looking like a drowned rat and feeling flat as a fart because of the battering my mind, body and feet had took today.

I was so longing for a hot shower but alas; I had to bed down for the night pretty much as I was. Wet wipes are a godsend at times like this.

My feet needed some serious foot maintenance after 13 and a half hours of walking through some of the worst weather and terrain. The pain was radiating through every inch of my feet with each heartbeat. I could literally feel my heart beating through my feet. Despite my feet being immersed in rain for most of the time I had been walking, the debris and stone was now deeply embedded in my open wounds.

I was so worn out and I felt a sudden cold and shivering feeling coming over me, as if I was experiencing the early stages of shock. I knew it was the effects of the day and having stopped walking, my body was cooling down.

My mind was entering dark places again. The demons were back with a vengeance and telling me to focus on the pain and all the reasons I should stop and go no further.

This was now becoming a daily fight in my head and one I was not willing to lose.

Day 6

Shap to Kirkby Stephen

After yet another night of torrential rain and discomfort with the pain radiating through my feet with every heartbeat, it was time to zone the tiredness and pain out with my morning mindfulness session.

These daily 10 minutes of meditation are my time to lock away from the world and get to a place where I can reframe my mind from what has happened in the past day and to prepare it for the day ahead.

Once my daily feet and skin splitting exercises were complete, and I gulped a caffeine boost down, it was time to head off on one of the longest parts of this adventure, a 20 miler to Kirkby Stephen.

I didn't even know what day it was as all days now seemed to blend into one, with the same punishment being dished out by the terrain on my feet along with the relentless weather. All I knew was it was 8.50am and time to get on the road.

The Lake District National Park was now behind me and I was now entering the Yorkshire Dales National Park meaning things should get better from here on in.

Heading up a backstreet path to pick up the main trail, I had to battle nettles as high as my waist and bite my tongue with the stings they were dishing out on my sore feet and legs.

Ian was ahead of me trying to create a nettle free path to help reduce the impact on me. Had he not been with me, I would do this myself and it would be like trying to carve my way through a jungle of nettles and stopping me in my tracks before the day had even begun.

The rain once again had stepped up a gear and began battering us. It's like the weather gods waited for me to begin my day and decided to turn the tap on me for a laugh.

Once I was free of this nettle jungle, I joined the main path through the fields and it wasn't long before we were once again intercepted by Rob Prance who was heading to Kirkby Stephen as his end point for the day too. He too was already looking battered by the weather and it was only a quarter past 9 in the morning. The forecast said this weather would be with us ALL day. Deep joy!

The noise of motorway traffic soon came into earshot as the M6 motorway got closer with each step. The mist and rain made for a grim start to the morning.

Heading over the bridge on the M6, I stopped and took a moment to observe the traffic all whizzing past below me. The motorway was awash with cars and trucks thundering away underneath me, all heading for their morning destinations. If I ever thought there was a "rat race" that we all get trapped in, this was it. Everyone was on a mission to get to work, deliver their goods, fight the traffic jams etc and the whole thing below me just felt so robotic and programmed.

Scarily though, despite the low visibility because of the rain, the number of cars that were racing down the M6 with no lights on to warn other road users of their presence was shocking.

Thankfully today, I was free of any confines of the "rat race" and the only restrictions I had were the ones I created in my mind.

Once over the bridge and back onto the path, Rob bid us farewell and headed off into the distance. He was walking faster than I could and I didn't want to be the cause of delaying him in this bad weather.

Weather aside for a moment, on a positive note, the landscape began changing for the better. The last 5 days have been some of the most challenging days I have ever had to deal with, and now on day 6 and the start of my transit through the Yorkshire Dales, the terrain was much friendlier, with more grassy field areas and paths that weren't covered in scree. The paths were still challenging with the stone, rock and dolomite but there were a lot more grassier "wins" to work with now.

By now the morning was in full flow and the familiar faces of groups of people transiting the Coast to Coast began to appear. They had all had their breakfasts in their cosy accommodation and were now tackling their day ahead too.

Heading across the grassy moorland up to a place called Seal Howe, and onto Crosby Ravensworth Fell, the groups of walkers began spreading out. Some small groups were huddled up checking maps, some were simply heads down and tackling the weather full on, just as I was at this point in time. The grass was like a sponge and every step oozed rainwater. Just like the mountains of the Lake District over the last few days, the ground was sodden.

Walking down from the fell and getting ever closer to a milestone point on today's journey, just north of a place called Orton at Gilt's Lane, Ian headed off to visit a place on the map called Robin Hood's Grave, a cairn situated on the fell itself North, North West of Orton. This is one of the many supposed burial sites of Robin Hood. Why here of all places? I couldn't tell you.

I continued on up the path as I didn't want to add unnecessary miles on to my very sore feet, walking with some Canadian travellers, one who was celebrating his 80th birthday this very day. He, along with his wife, were calling it a day at Orton Village to celebrate his birthday and make an evening of it with friends.

As I approached Gilt's Lane through the fields, Ian caught me up and showed me some pictures of Robin Hood's Grave as we walked. He was suitably impressed with it and I was wishing I had now experienced it for myself.

Walking down Gilt's Lane, the road was smooth(ish) and I found great comfort in the feeling under foot. The road surface was solid, smooth and not boggy like the grass I had been walking through and the cold surface provided a pleasant numbing effect for my poorly feet.

Two familiar faces were now walking down the road and catching up with me; it was Andy and his wife Anne who I had met on day 1 and subsequent early days on the adventure, both looking pretty beat up by the weather, just like the rest of us.

I stopped to chat with them both, knowing this would be the last time I see them on this adventure as they were taking a pit stop in Orton for the night and not continuing to Kirkby Stephen.

Walking down the road I saw the support vehicle some way off and this was an absolute blessing in disguise. I had been at it today for 5 hours in some horrendous weather; I was cold, wet, pissed off with the rain and for my feet not working properly.

I ducked out of the rain and sat in the support vehicle, dripping puddles of water on the floor whilst drinking a much-needed warm cup of coffee and eating a calorie loaded pasty.

Ian had already beat me to the vehicle and was trying to dry out his boots as they had become waterlogged along the way.

It was a struggle to get going again in the rain, but it had to be done.

There was still around 11 miles to go and it was already 20 to 2 in the afternoon so I needed to get a move on. Truthfully I could have just sat in the support vehicle all day but I knew the impact it would have on the overall adventure, so before the comfort set in I was zipping up my coat, topping my water bottles up, rubbing some Savlon on my open wounds, checking the map with Ian and then I was out of the support vehicle and back in the cold and wet.

Heading round to Sunbiggin and across Tarn Moor we caught a short break in the weather, allowing us to see the sun glinting off Sunbiggin Tarn in the distance. The weather was short lived though as the sky once again turned grey and the heavens released a torrent of rain on us once again. Being in the open and with no places to take shelter it was a case of just cracking on and riding it out.

With grass in abundance, the fells allowed me to increase my average barefoot walking pace to around 1.9mph, meaning that Kirkby Stephen was still in reach for the day's endpoint and I would have a buffer zone of a bit of daylight left should I come across challenging terrain that would slow me down.

Coming down from the hills onto the trails leading onto Kirkby Stephen High Street, I was so glad to be back into civilisation. Despite it being way after 9pm, it was still light and surprisingly busy with people milling around.

Having been to Kirkby Stephen many times I knew there was a cracking Chinese takeaway just off the high street and me and Ian made a beeline for it.

As I have become accustomed to when walking in a populated area, people began to do a double take as I passed them... had they really just seen what they seen? A guy wandering barefoot up the high street limping and looking quite broken? They sure had!

I asked the lady behind the counter in the takeaway if I was allowed in to place an order looking in the state I was, and she said "absolutely". I was so hungry, meaning I had to be sensible with my order as I would have ordered everything off the menu at this point. I was lacking in calories, needed a hot meal and a good sit down. I had after all been at it today for almost 13 hours. Having lived on pot noodles and pasties, having a Chinese meal meant me and Ian could feast like kings and the food not only gave me an energy influx, but a great boost to my overall mental state.

This was also one of the first proper nights me and Ian had time to chat about things so far. It's great how a simple thing like a Chinese takeaway, something people take for granted in normal situations, can have such a great impact in extreme circumstances.

Despite it being a very late finish, we surveyed the map for the next leg of the journey and me and Ian chatted openly about our thoughts on how this adventure challenge was impacting us both.

Mentally I kept quiet about things going on with my demons trying to force me to quit and so my chat was around things physically impacting me.. my feet, the terrain, the weather and so on. Ian was the same.

It had literally poured down all day long. It never let up once apart from a 10-minute reprieve over Tarn Moor.

Framing my mind to make sure it was ready to take on the next leg of the challenge, I embedded thoughts that this next leg would be the halfway point on the adventure in both miles and days. Many people think Kirkby Stephen is the halfway point on the Coast to Coast route because the railway station is there and it is accessible for people to get to and from it when in fact the official halfway point is a place called Keld, the place I was heading to tomorrow.

Kirkby Stephen to Keld will take me back into the hills and despite it only being a distance of 11 miles as the crow flies, I was gearing my mind up to accept that it may be a challenging leg of the journey under bare feet but one that is totally achievable.

After 20 miles and a 13-hour day, I was beat. I was in excruciating pain with my feet and found that if I relaxed with them in an elevated position, the pain would lose some of its intensity. Hopefully, this would help me get a few hours of uninterrupted sleep.

Day 7

Kirkby Stephen to Keld

The sleep I was hoping for overnight wasn't the 5 hours I wished I could have had. Stop start, I managed around 2 hours of sleep because of the pain in my feet. The pain was literally radiating throughout my whole body and making me feel sick. I was constantly moving around to find a position of comfort, only to have the pain override this each time I settled back down. Elevating my feet brought temporary relief, however this wasn't the answer.

The night dragged on and at first light I was up and trying to stop my feet from banging. After popping two ibuprofens, I poured some cold water on my feet to see if that would work. The cooling effect gave a temporary relief however it was only a matter of minutes before the throbbing returned. This pain was not going away.

After almost a week at my adventure challenge, was this it? Was this the end of the game for me? How was I going to tell everyone? The only people right now who knew how physically impacting my injuries were was my support team and even they had told me I should really think about what I was doing and pull out if I needed to.

I had to give my head a shake here as this was the defeatist demons talking again and getting into my head whilst the world slept. We all experience thoughts overnight where something so small is magnified into a big issue and has a tendency to keep us all awake with worry, and this I believe was now happening to me.

I was in pain, no denying that, however I was also sleep deprived and not seeing things as I normally would. Quitting was not an option.

I spent more time exercising my feet to loosen them up well before the barefoot walking day starting, after all I was wide awake and had a lot of time on my hands. The pain was not just from the cuts or the skin splitting on my feet anymore; it was now coming from deep within my feet.

The walking day started with a visit to the butchers on the high street to load up on pies, sufficient for the planned 10 hours ahead of me.

Heading out from Kirkby Stephen High Street, down across the bridge to the river, the rain was once again coming down hard. I paused for a picture at the signpost that read Coast to Coast, Robin Hood's Bay 108 miles. Wow... 108 miles is a long way, considering the other side of the sign says St Bees 82 miles. Is that all I had covered in 6 days? 82 miles.

Walking down the side of the river and out towards the quarry, the path was becoming very challenging under foot. This continued as I headed up Birkett Lane before veering off and onto the fells again where there were more grassy "quick wins" for me to walk on.

Intercepting us once again was Rob Prance. He knew we made it to Kirkby Stephen as last night when walking past one pub as I entered the high street from the hills, some guy outside of the pub shot inside and said to everyone in the room, including Rob "There's a bloke out there in bare feet just casually walking up the high street". Rob knew instantly who it was.

Rob walked with us for a while until a point where the path split off left, right and straight ahead on Hartley Fell. I, along with Ian wanted to visit the Nine Standards, up on the aptly named Nine Standards Rigg, however Rob wanted to miss these out so bid us farewell and headed off into the distance on the right-hand path.

The Nine Standards, as the name suggests, are nine awe inspiring stone cairns which have stood for centuries overlooking Kirkby Stephen and beyond, on the Pennines.

Evidence suggests these nine towering cairns, some more than 12 feet in height, were boundary markers between Yorkshire and Westmoreland with documents mentioning the Standards dating as far back as the 12th century. Other suggestions as to their existence were that they were Roman structures to deter the Scottish, however their real purpose remains a bit of a mystery.

Heading up the fell to the Nine Standards, you could make out the tops of them, all lined up on the top edge of the hill. At this point they were too small to see, however the closer I got to them, the more majestic they became.

You could be mistaken that there was an army looking down on you, so perhaps there is some truth about them serving a purpose to scare off the Scots.

Approaching the Standards, you get an overwhelming feeling as these man-made structures tower above you and standing by one; they appear to be perfectly lined up on the edge of the Rigg.

One thing I was warned about up here by Rob was the peat bogs. "Expect a bit of sinking in the path on the moorland as you leave the Nine Standards behind,", Rob explained.

He wasn't wrong!

After a 20-minute rest stop taking in the splendour of the Standards, it began to rain yet again, and that was my cue to leave these magnificent structures behind and head off across the moor.

With the Nine Standards behind me, the surrounding area that was scattered with scree and stone changed to a flat stone and then peat moorland, and once back on the official path it was waterlogged and my steps saw a brown water envelop my feet as the water was squeezed out of the peat bog below.

So far so good though. It didn't seem as bad as what I was told to expect, and with that, BOOM! the very next step saw me stuck in a peat bog up to my knee. It was like quicksand, pulling my leg further into the boggy moor and trying to hold me prisoner. Despite this, it was a cold and therapeutic feeling on my feet with the peat mud consistency squeezing through my toes and covering my wounds like a poultice.

I was stuck fast, and all Ian could do was piss himself laughing... that was until he took a step and ended up in it up to his thighs. Instant Karma?

After an hour and a half of tackling the peat bogs and only covering 2.5 kilometres, the terrain became firmer and allowed me to claw back lost time from sinking in the bogs with every step I took.

Coming off the tops and down Coldbergh Side towards the road there were 2 paths, and the map wasn't really giving us the information we needed at this point. In our wisdom we split paths, assuming they both led to the road where we needed to be, the B6270 Keld road. I took the left path over a stile in the wall and Ian took the right. One of us would have to connect back up with the other, but, one of us would get the right path, rather than both of us go one way and then have to double back.

Bugger!! It was me!

My "false" path took me to the bottom of the hill OK and then routed me to an old rusted Gate that was locked shut and had a wooden fence on the other side of it.

That's all I needed, climbing two gates in bare feet, especially with one of them rusted and looking in a total state of disrepair. Once over these hurdles, I came out at a point down the path to where Ian had ended up. It may have been a bit of effort from my side, but it was still a positive outcome.

The sun was now shining, and the grey and very miserable looking sky was gradually being replaced with a friendly blue sky as the afternoon wore on.

I was off the hills and now onto 4 miles of hard, bitty, stone chipping type road, and without the prospect of any immediate quick grassy wins I had to just bite the bullet and take the pain under foot.

It was tough going as each step felt like someone was turning a blunt knife into the soles of my feet. How I wished I was back in the peat bogs right now.

4 miles of road became a battle of mind over pain as I pushed on, grabbing the odd grassy bit here and there to give me maybe 10 seconds of reprieve. It's hard to describe how a road surface can cause so many issues, however at one point I even contemplated climbing back into the hills and find another way to Keld which would ultimately lengthen my day, just to get round these last few miles of road.

I was walking 100 metres, stopping, dusting off the stone chippings that were grinding into my feet, taking a deep breath and carrying on. It was torture. It was a case of walk, stop, clean feet, repeat.

Heading into Keld there was a field full of women camping ahead of me to the left. A car came out of the field and as it drove past me, a cigarette smoking woman hung out of the car window and shouted pure obscenities at me... nice girl. I bet her parents are so proud of how she has turned out in life.

Luckily, I have skin like leather and am used to the reactions of people who see me in the hat and bare feet, both good and bad. It used to phase me, but I stopped caring about it some time ago.

Having been on the road for over 3 hours I finally made it to the end point of the day at Keld. That last 4 miles on the road had broken me. I felt more pain from that road than what I did coming down scree filled trails in the Lake District. The tarmac had really seen my feet off today.

Knowing how broken I felt today, the support team picked me and Ian up and took us to Tan Hill so we could have some real food and a hot shower.

The new owners of Tan Hill, the highest pub in England, have installed outside showers for hikers, bikers etc to use which is great. When I say outside showers, I don't literally mean outside. They have created a shower and toilet room that visitors can use as they pass by.

Dan and Mick headed off to the pub whilst me and Ian got out of our stinking clothes. This alone was a struggle for me as every movement of my body seemed to jolt my feet.

I desperately needed a shower but the thought of the water hitting my feet was daunting. "At least the hot clean water will shift out some ingrained stone in the cuts and help remove some green puss weeping out of one of the open sores on a toe on my right foot," I thought to myself.

The water hitting my feet from the shower was too much to take and the pain of the hot water brought tears to my eyes. I desperately needed a shower; I normally love showers, being a bloke who has 2 a day and here I was hating every minute of it.

I sat in the bottom of the shower tray with the water hitting my head and cascading down my body and broke down in tears. The pain level in my body was now at the peak it had been since the start of the adventure and I was struggling with it all. Every day I was wrestling with dark corners, immense pain and the weather and had I been of fragile mind this would have been my "fuck it" moment where I threw the towel in.

Thankfully, I am of a stronger mind and can navigate my way through these lows.

I had people waiting in the pub for me, had Ian waiting back at the support vehicle and I needed to get myself together, so I didn't let these guys down.

This was my motivational anchor point that saw me snap out of the low place I had just hit, and wiping the tears away I had a last attempt at trying to prize out some foreign objects embedded in my feet, trying not to cause any more pain to them.

The shower gave me a mental boost and allowed me some private time to shift off the weight I was carrying on my shoulders. I was clean(ish), had a glowing warm feeling around me and was ready for a beer with the lads. Seven days ago I had set off on this journey, and tonight I wanted to switch it off and just chill and have some banter.

Being a Friday night, this was like a night out. Tan Hill was packed with people and thankfully the support guys had grabbed a table earlier on, otherwise it would have meant standing at the bar all evening, something my feet could not take.

I collapsed on a sofa in the back room of the pub and zoned out for a moment in time. Two people came over, shook my hand and said how they admired what I was doing, having heard about a barefoot guy doing the Coast to Coast. This gave me a great boost and a positive re-affirmation that continuing on with this adventure was the right thing to do.

Thankfully, I didn't need to get up all that much in Tan Hill, however on the times I did I could do nothing other than hobble around. My feet would not carry me anywhere effectively. They had seized up!

I needed a pee and had to hobble to the men's toilets barefoot. I would never dream of going into a men's toilet in bare feet normally, and even take measures to hitch my trousers up when I have to use a men's room when I have shoes on, to stop my trousers catching the dirty floors, so this was a new low for me. I had no option though. I needed to pee and had to bite the bullet and deal with it.

Sitting back on the sofa it was so good to know that the halfway point on my adventure challenge had been reached. I was almost 100 miles and 7 full days into the adventure, having battled and survived some of the shittiest weather and terrain I have ever known.

Day 8

Keld to Reeth

After another rainy night, I was up early and getting on with my foot exercises. Despite the luxury of a shower from the previous night, my feet still needed to be split open to allow more flexible movement. This was now my ritual first thing to do on a morning upon waking up.

Today's planned start time was 9am and given it was 5.30am, I had plenty of time to kill, so after my morning meditation I sat in a bit of a daze and not thinking about anything in particular, just letting my thoughts come and go. It was therapeutic for my mind to not fix on one thing and over analyse it.

My thoughts soon returned to my feet though as the banging pain reminded me they needed looking after. They now had free movement as best as they could, and it was time for the fresh open wounds to be tended to. First job, manuka honey foot cream to make the skin soften up more. Trying to rub the cream into my feet full of open wounds, sores and scabby bits had become an art and a science over the last few days, something I had become quite adept at.

My feet were full of debris and If I could get some embedded stone and grit out of the wounds before I started the day off, then I would without a doubt benefit from it. Unfortunately, though this was not meant to be. Trying to free off tiny stones from deep within open wounds was just too painful, so I figured they hadn't stopped me up till now and hopefully won't for the next week ahead.

One concerning factor was the toe on my right foot. Over the last couple of days, the wound on it had begun to weep thick green stuff and last night's shower was the first real attempt at getting it clean. Today it was back and weeping again. I applied Savlon and hoped it would seep into the wound enough to hold the onset of something nasty at bay.

By now the overnight rain had stopped and on checking the forecast for the day ahead, it was showing to be a sunny start which would eventually be swapped out with rain from dinner time, lasting the rest of the day. "It is what it is" I thought to myself. It is pointless getting hung up on the weather as there is absolutely nothing I can do about it, and after the last week, I have become used to it raining pretty much every day, anyway.

As the day continued to come to life, Keld was basking in beautiful early morning sunshine and it really epitomised what the start of a summer's day should be like, something that had eluded me pretty much each day up till now on this adventure.

I switched the satellite tracker on at 9am and after a quick check of things it was time to head off into the hills for the day as I made tracks to my end point, a place called Reeth.

Just after 9am as I began walking down the road with Ian, a car pulled up and out jumped our friends, Neil Appleyard, and his daughter Amy.

Amy had been itching to join us on a leg of this adventure and reached out asking to meet us today and walk the whole way from Keld to Reeth.

It's always great to have company on my adventures and so far, Ian has been a great support for me, having someone to chat with, have a laugh with, share the tough shit moments with, and especially in Ian's case, someone to have save my ass when needed.

Heading out from Keld, the trail was challenging under foot as I passed through West Wood and along Crackpot Hall. Crackpot Hall is a place of mystery and is situated on the Coast to Coast route, not too far from Keld. The location has housed a building since before the 16th century. The building occupying the area dates from the 18th century and is the ruins of what was once a two-storey farmhouse.

A couple walking the opposite way had heard about my barefoot adventure and asked if they could grab a quick pic with me before heading off on their travels. Happy to oblige, I stood with the folks while Ian took on the role of photographer and did the honours.

As the morning wore on, a feeling of anxiety was gathering pace and starting to come over me.

Here's the thing. I didn't have any explanation for it, nor could I stop it from coming on. My eyes began to fill with tears, and I was having to hold my breath to stop myself from just crying. What was happening to me? I knew I was in pain with my feet but not to the point where it was making me feel like crying without me even knowing why.

Psychologically I was battered, I just didn't realise it. The lack of sleep played a huge part in all of this, as did the immense pain and I guess for seven and a half days the effect had built up to a point where I could no longer control it. These feelings needed to fully come out, and this was the point in time it was to happen, on Buzzard Scar at 410 metres (1,345ft).

When the meltdown struck Ian, Amy, and myself were all at varying heights on the hill, with me being at the back. Initially Ian and Amy had no clue what was going on as they couldn't see the tears rolling down my face, however as the inner feelings gathered pace, my breath began to take on a pant and I took deep breaths to try to hide the onset of this uncontrollable meltdown.

Boom! It hit me like a baseball bat... Here I was halfway up a hillside, now standing with my head down on my walking pole sobbing my heart out uncontrollably.

Ian noticed and shot down the hill, as did Amy, and they both did their best to comfort me. I just couldn't stop crying. A pressure cooker effect had gone off with the stress of it all, along with the pain and sleep deprivation causing me to blow in spectacular fashion.

I had never been in a situation like this before in my life and I was struggling to handle it, let alone these two trying to help me manage it. It just needed to pass and work its way out of my system. There was literally nothing these guys could do to help me. I have never ever felt this low in my life. Looking back at the incident with the tears in the shower last night, it got me thinking they were the pre-curser to this blowout.

The way this event came on was weird. One moment I was fine and the next thing I knew was I was out of control of everything. As someone who is on the pulse in this life, I found this hard to understand and it felt very scary.

It took a while, but once my meltdown had passed and I had composed myself, I was back at it and feeling on top of the world, like a weight had been lifted off my shoulders. I was following Ian and Amy who were ahead of me because of my lower barefoot speed and the trail became more challenging as we headed up towards a footbridge at the old disused Swinner Gill lead Mines. On reaching the footbridge, the area became a technical scramble given the amount of rock and stone everywhere.

Having Amy with us was a godsend as I cut my foot open, and her being a nurse in training, she sorted it out with some good old cotton wool and TCP, something she had the foresight to bring with her, knowing my feet were a disgrace.

Applying the TCP on all my cuts and wounds bloody stung, but I knew things would be OK after this magic potion was applied to them. A hiker stopped and asked if I was OK whilst Amy was tending to my foot and I assured him all was fine. It's good to know that folk would stop and ask if all was OK and not just walk on as if nothing was happening.

By now the rain had returned, drizzle at first, before the now regular daily torrential pour. Was this rain ever going to stop? It was now becoming one of the wettest June's on record.

Heading over the moor and walking gingerly, trying to find grassy side areas due to the dolomite and stone covered path, we met a paramedic and his wife on the trail who looked at the mess of my feet and advised a 10% bleach to water mix for me to steep them in. He advised that the bleach would loosen and clean the debris out of my feet, and it is a method he has used successfully for treating motor bikers who ended up with gravel rash after an accident. It sounded like a plan to me and I was prepared to shoulder any stinging pain that came with the immersion of my feet into the hot bleach water if it meant shifting some ingrained stones.

The dolomite paths continued for miles, carving a route through the upper moorland. We decided to come down off the hill, head for Gunnerside and take the river path to Reeth as a walker told me it would be better on my feet at the bottom because of the abundance of meadow grass and a much flatter terrain.

Heading off the moor and descending into Gunnerside, I got hold of my support team via walkie talkie because of there being no 4G signal to make a call, to let them know what the paramedic had said, and they headed off and arranged the bleach and bowl for my feet.

Once out of Gunnerside, I was duly met with open, flat and soaked meadows, but I wasn't going to complain because it felt absolute bliss on my bare feet. Aside from a weird part of the trail where one minute you were walking through a beautiful meadow and then onto a cinder track type path, which then became a wall some ten feet in height with a drop into the field below, the trail levelled out for the rest of the way into Reeth.

After a ten-and-a-half-mile day and almost 11 hours at it we popped out on the green at Reeth where Amy's husband and daughter were waiting for her, and Dan from my support team was waiting for me and Ian.

After parting hugs with Amy and John, Dan drove us the 1 mile to a place called Grinton where we would stay the night.

In the local pub car park, the recommended 10% bleach/hot water potion was made up in a bowl for my feet to steep in. Before I could even get my feet in the bowl Dan and Mick scarpered over to the pub for a couple of pints, and to grab some seats for us all.

Slipping my feet into the bowl of bleach water wasn't as bad as I thought and apart from the smell of bleach, steeping my feet felt awesome. The bowl was only good for one foot at a time, so I steeped one for five minutes and then swapped it out for the other and swapped again. After 20 minutes of bleach water, my feet looked clean and some of the grit and debris had dislodged and disappeared. There was still a lot of ingrained and embedded stone and grit in the open wounds on my feet, however being so embedded this was likely to take some days to work free.

After getting changed out of my smelly clothes and having a wet wipe wash down, I hobbled over to the pub for a catch up with the support lads who were now stuffing their faces with burgers, and to have some food with Ian.

The owner of the pub was a very nice chap who knew about my adventure challenge and let me in regardless of having no footwear on, shaking my hand and even dropping a donation in to my charity box. Top bloke.

By now it was once again pouring down outside and I was wishing I could stay in the comfort and warmth of the pub, but unfortunately it was time to retreat for an evening of listening to the rain coming down hard again.

Once back in my own space and in the dark and cold, I began welling up again for no reason. The meltdown on the hill today was coming back into my thoughts. I knew this was the demons coming out to play taking full advantage of the thoughts of the weak moment I had earlier in the day and using them to try to convince me to quit.

My mind was feeling very fragile, but once again, quitting was not an option.

Day 9

Reeth to Richmond

I woke up after a few hours' sleep because of the now predictable and constant banging in my feet and not forgetting the torrential rain that had been hammering down all night.

On the surface of things, today was just another day as each day was blending into one and taking on a familiarity of rain, pain, sleep, repeat.

Counting the days since I started the adventure on my fingers, I realised it was Sunday the supposed day of rest. No chance of that I thought as I had 15 miles to complete as I made my way across the countryside to Richmond.

Today was no ordinary Sunday though, it was also Father's Day, and I was spending it away from the kids which made me feel a bit shit, but sometimes that's the price you have to pay when you're an adventurer.

As usual, I was up before everyone else so had time to think a lot about the journey so far, the up's and downs and the challenges I've faced. Yesterday's meltdown was still a prominent feature in my head and so were the thoughts of the days that still lay ahead.

Suddenly my phone vibrated as a text arrived from my daughter, Alyssa.

Now, being 14 and a half, it's rarely I get a text off my daughter (Texting your dad probably isn't the cool thing to do as a teenager), so my heart sank a little.

"Happy Father's Day Dad! I love you so much and I'm so proud of what you're doing right now. Keep going, you're almost there. Despite all the weather and the difficulties, I hope you're having a good time. Lots of love, Alyssa. x"

Fighting the tears after reading that message and not wanting her to know the impact the text really had on me, I replied *"Thanks Alyssa. That text means so much. See you all in less than a week's time..xx"*

Tears streaming down my face, I had to get my shit together before Ian surfaced from the support vehicle he was sleeping in and began preparing for his day ahead.

Should my eyes be puffy when the lads got up, my plan was to tell them I was having a bad bout of hay fever. "That would work," I thought.

I was hoping this was just emotion passing because I was missing the kids on Father's Day, and I prayed that it wasn't the meltdown from yesterday starting to rear its head again and trying its hardest to dominate my day from the outset.

Within an hour of Ian being up and about, and after two cups of strong coffee for the caffeine hit, we were back at Reeth at the point where we left off last night, ready for the day to start.

Running through the kit to make sure I had everything for the day ahead, a familiar voice from behind shouted my name. It was Rob!

Rob, too, was preparing for his day and planning to set off not long after we were. He saw me on the village green so came out of his digs to wish me and Ian well for the day ahead.

With the clock hitting 9am it was time for the satellite tracker to be switched on and to head off towards my destination of Richmond, some 15 miles away.

By now there was a small crowd gathering, inquisitive over my crazy hat and me having no shoes and socks on, wandering around on their village green. "Who was this strange guy?" they must have thought.

Setting off from the green, a few people initially walked with me and Ian, and on passing the Copper Kettle team rooms I met the lovely proprietor. After a quick photo outside of the tearooms and some kind words of encouragement from her, I continued down the road before branching off and heading across some fields to begin the journey to Richmond and leave Reeth behind.

The first main stop on the route was at a quaint little place called Marrick, as the BBC were intercepting me at that point to do some filming about my barefoot adventure and find out how it has been so far. From Reeth, Marrick was some 3 miles away, and I needed to get a move on as I was due there for 10.30am, meaning I had to walk a consistent 2mph.

Prior to my arrival, the BBC interviewed some hikers passing through Marrick on their own Coast to Coast adventure and it was only a week later when watching the segment back once I had finished my adventure, one guy called me stupid for doing the Coast to Coast in bare feet. Each to their own, I thought. The crew from the Beeb were brilliant and after around 45 minutes of filming and interviews, it was time to continue on with the journey to Richmond.

The sun was now beating down, and the forecast was saying it was set to stay like this for a good part of the day ahead before, you guessed it... the rain was to come back in.

Having spent most of this adventure under cloud and accompanied by heavy rain, it's surprising how a bit of sunshine can bring about a real feel-good factor. I find it helps give me more energy and drive to do things, even if at this moment in time my feet can't keep up with me.

After wandering through fields and trails, I began heading to a point on the route where I thought it would be good to stop for something to eat and take a 20 minute rest for my poorly feet when I was intercepted by Paul and Sarah Atchinson and their son, Charlie, a couple of miles outside of Marske, Richmondshire, and they walked with us back into Marske itself.

Over the last couple of months, Charlie has been out singing on a weekend in prominent places including Hartlepool, Durham City and Liverpool to help raise awareness of my challenge along with funds for the Chris Lucas Trust, one of the charities I support on all my adventure challenges. This little guy is destined for big things in life. At an age where most kids are playing on their game's consoles,

Charlie is out there and using his talents to help those kids and their families who are less fortunate than himself. This young man is only 6 years old, how good is that?

After a brutal walk down a steep hill on the Hard Stiles road, it wasn't long before I arrived at Marske, which is due west of Richmond. Little Charlie took his shoes and socks off to walk down this road with me in a show of support, but I convinced him to put them back on as this road surface was nasty and I didn't want it to hurt his feet.

Arriving in Marske, it signified I was now only 5 miles away from a major landmark on my adventure and the end point for the day, Richmond. Marske was also the perfect place to stop for a pot noodle and a sit down in the sun with everyone who was now walking with me.

Something happened next that I will be forever grateful for. Paul and Sarah knew I was experiencing a serious lack of sleep, and whilst I was shovelling a spork full of noodles in my mouth, they gave me the keys to their caravan, at Brompton on Swale, for the night. WOW!

I was literally bowled over with this kind gesture and with their generosity. The great thing here is Brompton on Swale was on my Coast to Coast route as well! "How good is this?" I thought.

A night of comfort meant I needed to walk on further than Richmond today, but an extra two miles would not be the end of the world, despite the pain in my feet. I had a new positive anchor in my head, an unexpected goal that would bring great benefit, including the chance of a shower so I would get to the end point at all costs and no matter what time of night I got there. The weather was forecast to bring heavy rain overnight into the area and having a dry, warm place to stay would be so welcomed.

Getting the caravan keys back to Paul and Sarah wouldn't be a problem either as they were coming to see me finish the adventure challenge in Robin Hood's Bay. I decided the safe bet was for Ian to take custody of the keys just in case I lost them. There was just as much chance that Ian could have lost the keys, but it made me feel better, ha!

Leaving Marske, it was flat going en route to Richmond and with the sun shining and banter flowing, me and Ian wandered and took the piss out of the world itself.

Popping out at civilisation in Richmond, after a challenging walk through Whitecliffe Wood because of the nature of the trail, it wasn't long before I was back on a road and the surface wasn't too bad for my feet.

Hobbling down the road, Richmond was in full view ahead of me.

My feet were very sore by now, having been at it for 9 hours. Over the last few miles, I had taken on a kind of Charlie Chaplin walk, which weirdly seemed to help ease things under foot.

In a bit of a zoned out place in my head, I was continuing my weird Charlie Chaplin walk down the road, stopping to look at a couple of vintage cars in a state of disrepair and wondering their worth, why the owner hadn't done anything with them and so on, when a figure jumped out of the passenger seat of a car parked a bit further down the road dressed in hiking attire and a woolly bobble hat.

Facing away from me I thought it was someone heading off for an evening walk, after all it was a lovely evening and the rain hadn't come back at this point. As the figure turned around, I realised it was my pal Sandra, her partner Michael and his son Mark who unexpectedly turned out to greet me and walk with me into Richmond town and give me a huge amount of moral support. It was another great boost seeing a friendly face I knew who had taken time out of their busy life to come and support me as I passed through their area.

Sandra had even prepared me a goodie bag of corned beef pie, chocolate bars, a can of cider and a can of pop to make sure I was getting some calories in me. This was so welcome and a big change from my diet of Pot Noodles.

Sandra walked with me as I entered Richmond town however nipped off with Michael to move the car and meet me at the other side of Richmond Bridge where I would head off to complete the last couple of miles for the day.

By now the filming I did earlier with the BBC had aired and people were tooting their horns and wishing me well as I was doing my weird wobbly walk through Richmond in my crazy hat and very sore bare feet. Support from total strangers (and friends) has been amazing on this tough challenge.

Heading towards Richmond Bridge I saw Sandra, Michael and Mark again and after a few hugs, it was time to veer off and pick up the public walkway that would take me to my end point of the evening. It was now 10 past 7, and the forecasted rain was back once again, but I wasn't bothered as it was creating a soothing effect on my feet, cooling them down and easing them up. I found a grassy area, sat in the rain with Ian, and divided the goody bag up and we feasted like kings.

The food we often take for granted in our normal day-to-day life can sometimes make a huge difference when all you have been used to for a week and a half is the good old staple adventure food, Pot Noodle!

Strangely, the rain never fazed us once as we ate.

After food, the plan was to continue on to Brompton on Swale Caravan Park to meet the support team who had gone over there themselves as they were aware this was the new endpoint of the day for us, before heading across the caravan park to the Atchinson's caravan for the evening to enjoy a night of comfort.

It was half past 8 when we made it to the caravan park and the pain in my feet was now beyond description, as by now I had been at it for 11 and a half hours. I was so dirty, covered in mud and the open sores were now bleeding into the mud.

I tried to use wet wipes to clean my legs and feet up and avoid a shower as I wasn't feeling up to it, but the mud and dirt just wasn't shifting so I had to find the strength and motivation to head off to the shower block to scrub up as best I could.

Getting undressed in the shower room was a struggle as I was very sore and pulling my shorts over my feet to get them off caused so much pain with the material brushing over the sores.

I pressed the water plunger on the shower and let it run to ensure hot water was coming through the shower head and then climbed in. I couldn't bear the pain of the hot water hitting the tops of my feet so had to do my best and shower all over whilst shielding my feet from the water. I ended up sitting in the shower's bottom base with my feet hanging out whilst giving myself a good hosing down. There's a first for everything in life and this was mine, sitting in a shower with my feet hanging out getting a good wash.

Limping back to the caravan brought the onset of shivers and the torrential rain wasn't helping the situation. I felt like a broken man. It took me around 10 minutes to walk the short distance from the shower block back to the caravan, a distance I would cover in less than 2 minutes under normal circumstances.

Unzipping the awning and walking inside, the rain sounded so angry as it beat down on the caravan. I didn't care though; I was finally safe and dry!

Despite being small in appearance, the caravan was warm and cosy, and best of all it had a TV in it. This was the first time I had seen any TV since Thursday the 7th June and whilst I wasn't interested in what was going on in the world around me as it would just be the usual stories of woe, I scanned through the channels for some comedy and came across Rude Tube which provided the laughs and to switch the day off on a fun note.

It wasn't long before I drifted off into a fantastic sleep. I had a roof over my head, and I felt safe.... For now!

The peaceful sleep wasn't to last though... Read on my friends.

Day 10

Richmond to West Harlsey

Listening to the rain pouring down on the roof of the caravan had a very soothing effect and helped me drift off into a wonderful sleep, the best so far on this adventure challenge. I felt safe, warm, and a million miles away from the outside world.

It wasn't to last though as my day started at 3.30am with Ian falling out of his bed and making the loudest bang I've heard. The sleeping area he was on in the caravan had moved during the night causing him to tip off it and land on the floor in total darkness resulting in me bolting upright, totally startled and wondering what had gone on. I thought we were being robbed!

I couldn't believe the best sleep I was having in over a week was prematurely brought to an end. Still, listening to Ian swearing and cursing made me piss myself laughing whilst he was bumping into everything in the dark. It was so funny to hear him trying to sort himself out. I was pleased at the same time that he was sufficiently away from me in the caravan that made sure when he fell; he didn't plant his ass in my face!

After a couple of hours of broken sleep once Ian had crawled back onto his bed, and his rant subsided, I was up and preparing my feet for the day ahead. So as not to disturb sleeping beauty, I headed off into the awning to run through my foot exercises.

Ahead of me today was a 23 miler with a planned end point of Ingleby Arncliffe, and I needed my feet to work to carry me there.

Movement of my feet was difficult, as overnight all the open sores had really scabbed up and the skin had become so taught. This must have been the effect of the dry air in the caravan I thought to myself. Doing my morning rocking exercises on my feet seemed more painful than usual and it took a while for the skin to split and release my feet from their trap. The scabs seemed to be solid today.

Just after 7am I received a message from the BBC asking if I was available for a live interview on the progress of my barefoot challenge. I always have time for my friends at the Beeb and within 10 minutes I was live and letting the region know my progress so far. I probably put a few people off their breakfasts as well when asked to describe the state of my feet. Yuk!

At this point on the adventure my feet looked like they had died and were just there for the sake of it. They had taken on a very off-colour looking tone overnight and some sores were now starting to look quite black.

After securing the caravan up and ensuring it was left in exactly the same clean state as we had found it myself and Ian began the (slow for me) walk across the caravan park to where the support team had parked up for the night and to grab a much-needed cup of coffee. After a bit of banter with the lads and a second, strong cup of coffee, it was time to head off and with a long day ahead, there was no time for breakfast, so it was a case of eating an energy bar on the way to kick my metabolism off.

Heading out of Brompton on Swale, the rain was stop start; However, the air temperature wasn't bad. The wet mud under foot was providing a soothing cushion to walk on and the cooling effect of the mud on my sores helped keep the pain in my feet to a manageable level.

Passing through a farm, the noise of the A1 was bellowing from the traffic and it broke the tranquillity of the countryside. To conquer the A1, I needed to walk down a very steep bank, so steep in fact I had to hold the fence with both hands as I made my way down it, to stop me slipping on my ass and ending up in a heap at the bottom. The path then went under the A1.

Once I was East side of the A1, I knew that I was edging ever closer to home turf.

Crossing under the A1, you could hear the traffic thundering along overhead. The tunnel path was full of stone chippings, making it slow going. Suddenly the walkie talkie burst into life and the support lads announced they had tipped up at the racecourse nearby and would I like a coffee? Would I?? Too right I would. A caffeine boost would be great now.

Leaving Dan and Mick behind, the route took us around the north of Catterick and you could hear a loud banging in the distance, like tank guns firing. "Was the military practicing today?" I thought to myself. To me it was the only plausible reason for the loud banging noises in the distance as they sounded fierce.

Following the trail down Flat Lane, we came out at a lovely place called Bolton on Swale. Waiting for us in his white VW Camper Van was Ian's brother Graeme who had been tracking our progress. It was fantastic to see him and for his words of encouragement.

Another car pulled up and came over to see us. It was a great fella called Jimmy Cummings, someone Ian, and I knew through our geocaching circles, and Jimmy too had been tracking our progress.

Both Graeme and Jimmy had come bearing gifts of energy drinks, cakes, and chocolate, which was gratefully received.

Given my feet were sore and tired today it was a great excuse to take half an hour out to chat with the lads, have some banter and rest my feet. These two stand up guys really had a positive influence on my adventure challenge. Whist taking this half hour rest, members of the public were pulling up in their cars, wishing me all the best for the rest of my journey too. "How good is that?" I thought to myself.

All too soon it was time to bid the guys farewell. I could have sat with them all day as the laughs were flowing, but I still had around 12 miles to complete before nightfall and it was now just after 2pm. Back on the trail, the sun was shining, and we were soon passing a place called Ellerton on Swale. Ian started telling me stories of his SCUBA diving days and how he and a few others had completed some inland dives in Ellerton Lake, and it sounded fascinating.

Despite being in the Coastguard for 20 years, I was a shit swimmer and had only ever tried diving once before on one of those try dive sessions and I just couldn't get away with it. As a nose breather predominantly, I found it hard to concentrate on sucking air through my mouth and constantly tried to breathe through my nose. I put the session down as a "tried that" in life. I enjoyed being a member of the diving club more, for the social aspect of it all. I didn't need to dive to still have a beer and a laugh with everyone in the club.

The next predominant landmark I needed to get to on the map was Danby Wiske, a quaint little village with a population of around 350 people.

It was a splendid early evening with the sun shining down on Danby Wiske, baking it in a golden colour. I can't ever remember being here in my life and my impression of the place made me look at the properties around me and question their worth, as it would be a lovely place to live.

Entering the village from the track through the fields, we headed north up the road and direct to the White Swan, a quaint 17th century pub.

Approaching the pub, I saw a white VW Camper van parked outside. It was Ian's brother Graeme's. He intercepted us earlier at Bolton on Swale and hung around at Danby Wiske till we arrived. Ian went into the pub to see if the landlord had any issues with me coming into the property looking all dishevelled and scruffy, however being a sunny evening, I prepared myself for sitting outside in the evening sun in the event of me being refused. I needn't have worried though, as the landlord was very accommodating and invited me in.

Graeme bought me and Ian a pint and I have to say it tasted fantastic. It was cold, crisp and wet, just like it's portrayed in the TV ads. At this point it was the best pint of lager I have ever tasted, or at least it felt like it.

The pub was full of weary hikers all completing the Coast to Coast and we exchanged stories of our journey so far. In the bar were some lovely people from Australia who took a shining to my hat and who were bowled over by my journey.

I met a very significant person in my life; James Barker, for a beer in the White Swan Inn. I have so much respect for this man and it was an honour to have him travel out to meet me and buy me and Ian beer. His words of encouragement really gave me a boost.

In the time I was in the White Swan I only had 2 pints, but it felt like the lager had given me wings! I felt revitalised and had a warm glow around me. I had to get out of the pub though or it would have turned into a full on beer session and I couldn't afford to take time out of the adventure if I was to make it to the end point at Robin Hoods Bay in my predicted timeframe, nor could I contemplate walking barefoot tomorrow with a stinking hangover and having to try to make up miles of lost time.

Leaving the White Swan behind, walking down the road I met some Danby Wiske locals, Rich Hampson and his son Oli who heard of my barefoot adventure challenge via the BBC TV story and they came out to wish me good luck as I was passing their doorstep. One thing I have noticed on this adventure challenge is the amazing spirit and support of complete strangers I have met along the way. After a good chat with them both and a few pictures for social media, I thanked them for their support and bid them both farewell. A bit further down the road, I was stopped by a couple more locals who wished me all the best. What a friendly place Danby Wiske was, "I could definitely live here," I thought to myself.

Given the time was now half past seven and there was still 6 miles of trail ahead of me if I wanted to make Ingleby Arncliffe before dark, the sensible decision was taken to press on until the light was lost, and that would then become the end point of the day.

It's impossible to safely walk barefoot in the dark and I didn't want to try it. All it would mean is tomorrow becomes a longer day to make up for any loss in mileage today.

Passing through a few farms and the tracks associated with them became a late evening challenge.

Walking ahead of me, Ian was on the phone to his missus, Sue, and he was trying to describe the state of my feet to her. Next thing, Ian passed his phone to me and Sue started kicking my ass at the state of my feet and said if she hears any more future adventures are involving my bare feet, my ass would be kicked again for real!

I don't mess with Sue; She is a great lass; However, she packs a wicked punch and I've been on the receiving end of one on many occasions.

Navigating through farms, I was tired and trying to dodge as much farmyard slurry as I could, given I had open sores on my feet, whilst taking it easy on the harsh paths and trying to find the best way through them.

I kept walking till 10 past 10, having completed a long 14-hour segment of my adventure, and my body and mind was now telling me it was time to call it a day.

The late summers evening light was fading fast, and my feet were extremely sore. Ingleby Arncliffe was so near being only 2 miles away, but still so far away now the darkness was descending.

My end point became Long Lane, just outside of West Harlsey, a little over 2 miles from Ingleby Arncliffe. Was I disappointed at not achieving my end goal? No, "it is what it is," I thought to myself. I had met some wonderful people today and whilst taking time out had a bit of an impact on my mileage, there were no regrets.

I still completed 21 miles today and managed to have two pints in a lovely part of the world en route, with some great people. This was a very positive end to my day.

Day 11

West Harlsey to Clay Bank

Picking up from where I left off on Long Lane, just to the north of West Harlsey, after losing the last glimmers of daylight last night, I headed down the farm track past Wray House that would eventually lead me through the countryside trails and to the busy A19 road.

It was at this point on the adventure that I came across some of the worst farm tracks I have walked on to date on this adventure. I have tackled scree paths in the Lake District, rough-and-ready farm tracks in the Yorkshire Dales, even the horrible track around Ennerdale Water, yet less than 60 miles away from the finish, I hit probably the worst farm track I have had to tackle to date.

I say the worst farm track as you need to remember I was tackling it barefoot. To someone in hiking boots, this would have been a dream path with loads of sharp grip under foot.

For me, however, this was absolute torture. Every step taken on this crushed stone track created a nauseous feeling and a pain level beyond comprehension. I couldn't even grab a quick win from some grass here and there as there was literally none. The sharpness under foot extended between both the left and right fence lines. Fair play to the farmer for providing and maintaining this public right of way but it caused me some slow going, in fact, my average walking speed dropped to less than 1mph at this point.

I felt like this track would take forever to get down. Thankfully, my walking pole helped take some pressure off my feet as my weight bared down on each step, making it feel like I was forcing my feet uncontrollably into the ground.

I had to swap the pole into opposite hands every few steps to give each of my feet a temporary break from the full weight bearing down on them with each step I took.

Thoughts to self... "Why didn't I have two walking poles with me today?"

Once clear of the farm and a few more brutal stone tracks, the ground became more friendly with a mix of grass/stone thrown in to the mix. The grassy bits at least allowed me to get my average speed back up but even then, this was peaking at a paltry average of 1.8 miles an hour because of a combination of the terrain and the sheer numbing damage to my feet on the earlier tracks today.

Each step was taking me closer to a point on the journey I was dreading and had been dreading since the planning stages of the challenge; the A19. The A19 is a very busy dual carriageway and an alternative road artery to the A1 through North Yorkshire, Teesside and Wearside.

As I approached the inevitable, the tranquil sound of the countryside was gradually being phased out and replaced with the noise of motorway traffic.

Ian went ahead as he saw some locals and he wanted the opportunity to quiz them and see if there was an alternative route in any way that crossed the A19 without having to walk across it at a busy time of the day like it was now.

I eventually caught up, and Ian delivered the news I was expecting. I had to cross the dual carriageway and just hope for the best.

Armed with this news, I wished the locals good day and then I was off down the final rough and dirty path that was to bring me right out at the unprotected northbound side of the dual carriageway.

Cars and trucks were thundering past and the wind from them reminded me of the dangers I now had to work with at this crucial point of my journey.

Crossing this dual carriageway was a real arse nipping experience, and for a bloke with very sore, and bare feet, having to dodge motorway traffic across 2 lanes northbound to reach the central reservation and then having to do it all again across both lanes southbound, it wasn't what I would describe as fun.

After what seemed an eternity of waiting nervously as cars and trucks raced past me, a gap between the traffic appeared that we judged as sufficient to allow me to hobble across the north-bound side of the dual carriageway to the central reservation, and with that I set off with Ian to get to this relatively safe point.

I had literally made it across to the central reservation with seconds to spare before feeling buffeted by the wind from a truck in the fast lane as it overtook another. That was a close shave!

The central reservation had now become a gathering point as there were hikers crossing the carriageways in the opposite direction to where I had just been. My barefoot adventure bemused them, and they began asking questions on how it's been, were my feet sore, where I'm heading to today and so on, all the while I'm stood shitting myself in between northbound and southbound carriageways while traffic was tear-arsing past me. I kept the answers pleasant but brief and as soon as a sufficient gap in the traffic appeared southbound; I ran! The pain in my feet was immense, but it was a far better trade off to going slow and being knocked over.

I still can't believe that on an official walk like the Coast to Coast that the public are simply allowed to stroll across a main dual carriageway, dodging trucks and cars, all of which are travelling at great speed. Even tackling the A1 yesterday, there was a provision of a walkway under the busy motorway to allow walkers and cyclists to cross in total safety.

Once across the A19, I could breathe a sigh of relief and take a quick pit-stop to rest my feet. Running across the southbound section of the road to get to safety had caused the pain in my feet to intensify, and it felt like this pain was travelling from inside the arch of my right foot to my knee.

Soon I was passing the quaint village of Ingleby Arncliffe and through its little brother Ingleby Cross. Over the years these two lovely villages have almost unofficially merged into one village with Ingleby Arncliffe being at the top of the hill, and you guessed it, Ingleby Cross at the bottom. The old A172 used to be the separation point of the two villages, but this road has been relocated and now bypasses this part of the village. Both villages are very old, old enough to get a mention in the Domesday book and still have standing buildings dating back to the 16th Century.

History lesson over, these days the villages are known as a gateway to the North Yorkshire Moors and for a fab pub!

Heading up the road, passing Arncliffe Hall and into Arncliffe Wood, the terrain became difficult under foot once again. The road went from a solid surface scattered with stones to one of a grey sharp stone, similar to what I experienced earlier in the day. Boy, this was tough going as not only was it bloody painful; I was also heading up a hill into South Wood requiring me to dig in with my feet to propel myself up the height. Not a good combination!

Having done this frequently in the early days as I transited the Lake District, I just bit the bullet, accepted in my mind that it was something I must deal with and "it is what it is".

I kept thinking to myself that it won't be long before I pick the Cleveland Way up and I would be on to more manageable trails under foot as these are more established paths. My average speed once again at this point was around 1mph.

Once established on the Cleveland Way and continuing to gain height with each step I took, the trail became more bearable as it changed from knife like stone everywhere to one of mud, grass and stone.

Just before the terrain levelled out, I needed to pee so stepped off the trail and into a bush (as you do). Once sorted I popped back out of the bush and straight into the path of a trail runner who must run these hills every day given, she was nowhere in sight before I stepped off the path to water the plants! I don't know who shit themselves more, me or her!

I still think about what she must have thought when a guy in a crazy hat, sunglasses and bare feet just sauntered out of a bush before the summit of a hill. Her face was priceless, but then again, I bet mine was as I wasn't expecting her to be there.

I'm not sure of her speed when she was running up the hill to our point of interception, however seeing her tear arse away like she did after our encounter you would think she was Usain Bolt.

Continuing my walk to the ridge top along the eastern edges of the wood, it wasn't long before some spectacular scenery came into view across the Vale of Mowbray. I couldn't believe I had walked barefoot through the areas I was now seeing way off in the distance.

The path on the ridge top of the woods felt coarse under foot. A few days earlier this would have been great to walk through in bare feet as it's made up mainly of mud, however a couple of days of decent sunshine has seen it dry out and become coarse, sharp and cracked.

One of the noticeable man-made structures ahead of me on the ridgeline to the left was the Wireless Transmitting and TV Station. Visible from the roads below and all around the area, this site has a multitude of aerials and microwave dishes all protected by huge a metal fence that screamed "Keep Out!". I stared through the fence and wondered how much radiation the whole transmitting station kicked out through its mass of aerials. "It must be safe," I thought, as the Cleveland Way goes right past the security fence and carries many a hiker daily past it.

Leaving the aerial site behind, I continued on the ridge top along the Coast to Coast path and could now see Teesside in the distance. "I live over there,"; I thought to myself as I tried to pick noticeable places out.

This began my thoughts of home and how in a few days' time I will leave this adventure behind me and transition back into the swing of daily life. Would it be the same after this adventure? Would I be able to walk the same again after this adventure? Would I have to take time out of life to recoup? Would my mind be able to keep the dark points I have experienced on this adventure at bay?

One thing I knew for sure, my feet would welcome the end of this adventure.

Carefully manoeuvring my sore feet over a stile and continuing on the Cleveland Way which the Coast to Coast route incorporates, I was off onto Scarth Wood Moor, beginning my journey over the North Yorkshire Moors, the third and last of the three National Parks I was to transit through on this journey.

Scarth Wood Moor is a relatively flat gateway to the open moorland ahead.

Ahead of me and getting taller with every step as he wascoming towards me was a huge guy with a bush hat on. This guy must be at least 6 foot 9 I thought to myself as I peered at him through my sunglasses... maybe even taller! Me being 5 foot 8, this guy was a giant.

As he was now within talking distance on the path, I wished him an obligatory and friendly "Afternoon!".

His reply, in what I had now established as a strong Australian accent was a simple "You look like a proper dick head mate".

If I've ever (and it's rarely) been stuck for words, this was the time. I didn't see that reply coming at all!

OK, this guy must have been weighing me up as he walked towards me... here's a bloke walking to-wards him in a crazy hat, sunglasses on, looking like a tramp with no shoes and socks on. I get the fact he may not see many people like me on a trail, but "Dick Head"?????

Did I mention he was huge? There was no way I was going to argue with him, so I just pressed on. I bet my average speed even went up as I worked to put a bit of distance between us both.

Ian was ahead of me at the time of this happening. However, when I caught up to him, he said, "Did that guy call you a dickhead?" "Yes mate, he did!"

Being back in "semi" civilisation, I had full 4G signal on my phone and it wasn't long before the peace and tranquillity of being surrounded by nothing but open moorland and blue sky was interrupted by a friend messaging me. Howy Soper had been tracking my progress via my satellite tracker and as he was on a half day's holiday from work, he came and intercepted me and give me some moral support. He was still a way off at the other end of Scarth Wood Moor, having pulled his car into a layby just after the point where the Cleveland Way route comes out onto Coalmire Lane, the moors road between Swainby and Osmotherley.

By now, my water bottle was running low, and I literally had a few mouthfuls left to last me until I next saw the support team.

Based on previous days' water needs, I carried the same amount of water that I thought would see me through, however, previous days comprised of flatter terrain and wetter days, not like the hot day I was experiencing today or the steep climb on to the ridge and open moor that I had just done.

To preserve water, I opened my bottle, put it to my mouth and let the remaining water hit my lips to moisten them and give a feeling of hydration, no matter how small it was. I figured if I moistened my lips then I was kind of doing something beneficial for my body and rationing the supply of water.

Ian had also run low on water so we couldn't even pool our resources.

By now the trail had opened up into big flat boulders, making it very easy to walk on and while we were beginning our descent off Scarth Wood Moor, a thin figure was walking up the trail in dark sunglasses, t-shirt and a plume of vape smoke. I said to Ian, "That's Howy for sure."

Sure enough, it was Howy intercepting us and the first thing I asked was whether he had any water with him? Unfortunately, he didn't.

Ian went ahead and descended to the road at the bottom where Howy had his car parked to see if the support team were around and happening to intercept us.

My pace was considerably slower than the normal walk Ian was doing, however on descending the steeper side of the trail to the road, I could see Ian chatting to a guy who looked vaguely familiar. Getting closer I realised it was an old pal of ours Geoff Leighton, who was visiting family in Swainby and came out and intercept us off the satellite tracking signal as he was nearby.

This was a great excuse for a pit stop to rest my sore and inflamed feet. The sun was also beginning to burn the tops of my feet now so chilling out in the shade was a must.

I shook Geoff's hand, and we exchanged pleasantries with him declaring I was mad for what I was doing, and how it was great to see both Ian and me. Ian had already beaten me to it to ask Geoff if he had any water and whilst he didn't, he offered to jump in his car and get some.

The lack of water was making me feel light-headed, so this offer was an absolute godsend. Whilst Geoff was away I had a good catch up with Howy who was telling me how he ventured over to see me when I set off from Kirkby Stephen days earlier but the lack of 4G signal in the area at the time made it impossible for him to track me accurately, resulting in him missing me as I headed out into the hills that day.

Within 15 mins, Geoff was back, and he opened his boot up to an Aladdin's cave of drinks and food. Not only were there bottles of Lucozade, but there were scones too! BIG scones with fruity bits in them as well! What a top bloke. I was so thirsty, but mindful at the same time that there was still a considerable way to go to the next rendezvous point where the support team would be waiting, and the drinks had to see me through.

After chilling with Geoff and Howy for half an hour, it was time to get sorted and head back off on the Cleveland Way and onto a familiar path.

12 months previously, both myself and Ian completed the Lyke Wake Walk, a gruelling 40-mile, old coffin trail walk across the moors. The challenge with this walk is it has to be completed in a maximum of 24 hours... we did it in 17 and at the time I had a knackered knee, an injury sustained from a previous big adventure! The Lyke Wake Walk starts at Osmotherley and finishes at Ravenscar, making for a west to east traverse of the North Yorkshire Moors.

The trail we were embarking on now is the same trail, difference is this time I had no shoes on so I knew what to expect and how it would be slow going.

We said our farewell to Geoff and Howy and crossed the road and headed off into Clain Wood.

Clain Wood is woodland area that the Coast to Coast path, Cleveland Way and the Lyke Wake Walk all share. Wooden posts and side marker stones show the route, the Cleveland Way with its white Acorn on black, the Coast to Coast with a blue arrow on white and the Lyke Wake with painted LWW stone inscriptions.

The terrain under foot was sharp given there were bits that had fallen off the trees, forest path and stones all over; It was your typical woodland path. Despite walking in a forest, there weren't many "quick wins" with grassy areas. My average speed once again as predicted slowed considerably as I navigated my way through the dense wooded area.

In a clearing near to where the path drops towards a dismantled railway, there is a stone memorial in memory of Bill Cowley. Bill Cowley was the person who devised the Lyke Wake Walk. After taking a moment to pay my respects and thanks to Bill, I continued down the path.

Continuing along the Cleveland Way at a pace of 1.8mph which had been my walking average throughout the adventure so far, I descended Carlton Bank to Raisdale Road. By now it was early evening, and I thought it would be good to take a pit stop on the descent and film a short social media update for the many people following the adventure. Within seconds, the likes and comments were coming in and these gave me a huge boost. People were supporting me from the comfort of their homes and following the adventure as it was happening. I needed this boost as I still had a long way to go, 3 and a half miles in fact, incorporating a lot of up and down of hills, taking in the spectacular Lordstones and Wainstones and my feet were already approaching my daily max.

As the days have passed on this adventure, I began to notice the warning signs when my feet are coming to the end of their daily life with the pain levels reaching max-point, radiating through my ankles and up to my knees. These warning signs happened in very inappropriate places sometimes, where I just can't stop and give up, meaning I have to squeeze out every drop of energy and gusto from my feet, push through the immense pain and battle with the switch in my mind that was trying to shut me down and give up for the day, and possibly the adventure.

On crossing Raisdale Road and cutting through the Lord Stones Country Park, people who were out and about for the evening with their dogs and friends began doing a double take as I wandered past. I could literally read their minds... Capital letters "WTF?" going through their heads at what they had just seen.

Most people stopped in their tracks and just looked in disbelief as I hobbled past to pick the Cleveland Way trail back up and climb out to the boundary stone and vantage point.

One guy dressed in tweed and wellies walked with me up the hill and chatted for a while before veering off to the right and heading back down from where he came. He was a nice chap. A bit of a country gent but very down to earth.

I found his company, along with Ian's, a great diversion to the trail I was now on, whilst I walked up to the ridge and vantage point. I was taking advantage of the grassy areas as best as I could as I also knew, given the distance I still had to do, along with my average speed, this would end up being a very long day so any timed gained through increasing my speed would be a bonus.

The path towards the Boundary Stone and vantage point suddenly opened up from rough trail and grass and into flat stones, big ones at that, and I could take full advantage of this barefoot friendly terrain as I made my way up the hill to the ridgeline. I knew things would flatten off for a while once on the top and assuming the terrain was kind to me, I could get a bit of speed on and shave a bit of time off my day. Even raising my speed on average 0.2mph would give me and my feet a reprieve today.

After a few difficulties transiting the hills, I soon had the magnificent Wainstones in sight, signifying that my day would end roughly a mile after I clear them.

The Wainstones are a bunch of huge weathered stones that date back way before the Bronze Age. You can see carvings on some stones showing cup and ring markings.

The Coast to Coast path cuts through these majestic stones with the trail being paved on the steeper parts; great news for my feet. The late evening sun was still shining and, in the distance, I could make out Teesside. Once again it got me thinking of my life over there and wondering what everyone was doing right now? It was one of those moments we all experience where the late sun is still shining and casting a golden glow across the land, allowing you to see for miles. A total feel-good factor!

Facing the Wainstones there was 2 paths. One to the right was a scramble through the middle of the huge stones and one to the left, which looked lazy. Ring a bell from day two on this adventure when I was at Ennerdale and ended up getting rescued from the side of a mountain?

You are right in thinking I took the left, lazy path around the stones which led me on a very thin path and a steep drop to the left below.

My heart began pumping and my arse started nipping. This wasn't good in bare feet and after a long day at it, I was lethargic, and my decision making wasn't as sharp as it was a few of hours before.

Where was Ian? Well, he took the "real way" to get through the Wainstones.

I could now see the main path 20 feet above me and to get to it I had to climb a steep muddy cutting on the hill's side. In hiking boots this would be a challenge; However, with tired, hurting bare feet and nothing to grab onto, it wasn't a good situation to be in.

I was now taking steps up this cutting in the hillside and with no grip on my feet I was just sliding back down. I eventually got so far up and felt the trusty hand come over the top once again, grab the loop in my backpack and drag my arse to safety. After a few wise words and expletive sentences from Ian that I just cannot put in this book, I dusted myself off, took a moment and carried on.

This fuckup 2.0 was nowhere near as scary as the magnitude of things that happened on day two, but scary enough to make me shit myself... AGAIN!

I am an advocate of following the path less travelled to enhance the adventure experience; But there is a lesson learnt here... think twice if you are in bare feet!

Leaving the Wainstones firmly behind, the focus was now on getting to the rendezvous point of Clay Bank to meet the support vehicle and put an end to this very long and painful day.

The two-way radio burst into life with Mick from the support team letting us know he was at the agreed rendezvous point and that we didn't have far to go.

It was tough and very slow going as I descended the path to meet the B1257. The terrain became sharp, jagged and so bad under foot; The pain in my feet was once again making me feel sick.

The roof of the support vehicle came into sight as I was descending and I knew that within a few hundred steps, day 11 was now complete.

Day 12

Clay Bank to Glaisdale Rigg

Overnight the skin on the top my feet had dried to a solid, crisp like texture that split open like a broken meringue the moment I started to try to walk on them.

By now I was used to this, but never being impressed with it as when the skin ripped open, it was bloody sore! 12 days in and I fully accepted this was now part of my everyday on the adventure.

After my morning ritual of massaging manuka honey foot cream into the tops and soles of my feet, I began to wake them up with the usual exercise of heel to toe movements. Pushing the heel up and shifting the weight onto the toes and vice versa seemed to get the blood flowing around my feet, and whilst it took about half an hour of these exercises for me to get my feet working, it was worth it.

By the time I set off from Clay Bank at 6.51am, my feet were allowing me to walk again. It may have been a hobble kind of walk, but it was still a walk.

The weather was a complete contrast to the sunny, warm day yesterday. The cloud was on the ground; It was teaming down with rain to the extent that you could see it hitting the road surface and bouncing back up.

The temperature had also taken a plunge during the night, making for a grim start to the twelfth day of this extreme adventure. Today were the perfect conditions for getting hypothermia in the hills if I wasn't careful, something I wasn't taking for granted.

I dressed in multiple layers and packed a reserve coat into my backpack as I knew through studying the forecast whilst exercising my feet, this weather was predicted to get a lot worse before clearing up early in the afternoon.

Having walked this route many times, I knew the first part of this journey to Blakey Ridge today would be relatively straightforward, even with bare feet.

Heading through the gate and up Carr Ridge, the easterly side of Urra Moor, it wasn't too long before I was on the ridge top, as the path comprised of flat rocky slabs, making it so easy to walk on.

I hadn't been walking 10 minutes and already I could feel the cold setting in to my feet.

By now the rain had become fierce and angry with the increase in wind velocity, and the visibility dropped further, meaning that 20 feet away from me, I was losing sight of Ian.

The first milestone of the day was Blakey Ridge, and that was around 9 miles away, and this weather was set to stay with us all the way.

Once on the top ridge, the path changed from slabs to a stone/grit, however, there was grass on each side of the path helping me out as the path itself was now feeling harsh under bare foot and toe curling in places when nature forced me on to it.

Where grass disappeared, I tried to use the bracken as a cushion on my feet, but I don't know what was worse, the coarse roots of the heather and ferns or the grit path? Either way, both were not ideal but as you have heard me say so many times on this adventure, "it is what it is" and there's nothing I could do about it other than press on and figure it out.

Thankfully, the terrain was quite flat with little ascent and descent, allowing me to average a steady 1.8mph.

The weather by now was driving into me and Ian at a rate of knots, and with 4 and a half miles to go till we reached the shelter of the Lion Inn, we were very exposed on the moor. Some days earlier in the Lake District we had experienced heavy rain and strong winds in the mountains but today was different, there was a wind chill with this and I could feel my core temperature starting to drop as my "waterproof" coat turned out not to be that waterproof, and had been allowing the relentless rain in, which ended up soaking through my layers, effectively creating a fridge effect.

I rarely hear Ian complain about the weather, as our search and rescue training taught us to tolerate and put up with all kinds of weather, but to be mindful of the effects exposure has on our minds and bodies.

Today was different though.

Ian was vocal about the weather and at one point said he was not sure he could make it to the Lion Inn at Blakey Ridge as he was feeling slightly hypothermic with the weather that was beating the shit out of us at this point. If the forecast was to be believed, we still had 3 hours of this to bear.

One thing they teach us in survival situations is to look out for the warning signs of hypothermia and I was seeing them appear, especially now Ian was opening up on how the weather was affecting him.

It was more important than ever now to get off this moor and into shelter, however there were no safe places other than the Lion Inn, by now some 2 miles away.

Ian's coat too had breached water in, and he was soaked to the bone, creating the chill effect.

We decided now was the time to take a minute and get spare kit out of our backpacks and put it on, meaning in my case, 2 waterproof coats and a fresh under layer. This immediately made me feel better and helped the psychological situation.

At times like this it is important to keep your wits about you as a very cold, wet and run-down body will inevitably lead to your mind making all kinds of mistakes and bad judgement calls.

The weather continued to berate us and at one point I began praying in my head to God, asking him to tell this weather to "Piss right off" and cut us some slack.

Given the situation, thoughts of pain in my feet were now secondary to the weather hammering down on us. I told Ian to walk ahead, with the assurances I would not slow down any further from my current rate of mph. I was using every spare bit of grass verge and heath to ensure I was away from the path which would cause my mph to slow down, something that I just didn't want to do right now. At one point, I began running on the grassy bits until I landed my feet on some sharp stone that hikers had kicked to the side from the path.

This stopped me in my tracks momentarily as I dealt with the sudden painful shock to hit my body.

In the distance I could see a brick building and I knew this was our safe haven.

It wasn't long before the path broke to the left and within 10 minutes, our time on this part of today's journey would come to a close.

As we walked up the stony, muddy path that wraps around the back of the Lion Inn, Mick Jorgeson, who was supporting us today, had walked out down the path to intercept us. We didn't know he was coming to intercept us at the time, he just appeared out of the mist and low cloud. It was that bleak I didn't even see the Blakey Howe Monument, a boundary stone on Blakey Howe, overlooking the Lion Inn. You can't normally miss it!

Mick knew the situation we had been in on this moor crossing, and after checking in on the two-way radio when we were within range, he had arranged a nice pot of sweet tea for us once we tipped up at the Lion Inn. Top bloke!

First things first, I had to get all this soaking wet clothing off and sort my feet out at the same time.

I have no shame at the best of times and stripping down to shorts and a t-shirt in a pub surprisingly drew very little stares, but then again it was just before the lunchtime rush so there weren't many people in at that point to stare at me.

I went to the bar and ordered three baked potatoes loaded with savoury toppings for Ian, Mick and myself. I'm not a fan of baked potatoes; However, today it seemed like the most energy giving warm food on the menu, and that was good enough.

I was rearranging my soaking wet clothes over some chairs when a couple of people came in, looked at me, looked at my feet and said "oh my god, are you the barefoot guy?" and after confirming I was he, they said they were hoping to bump into me on the crossing and that so many people had told them about me.

A guy in shorts and a t-shirt probably wasn't the best first impression I could make to these folks; However, it was better than being naked; I suppose.

After devouring the baked potato and steadily munching on the extra bowls of chips I ordered, my thoughts turned to the afternoon and the rest of the day ahead. We were pretty much halfway and given the comfortable surroundings, I could have literally called it a day at the Lion Inn and stayed in there the rest of the day, but I knew I couldn't. I had deadlines to meet and people coming out to see me at the finish line, so I needed to get there at all costs.

Dan, the film guy had now turned up and helped himself to the rest of the chips in the bowls and chatted about a few places he could intercept and film us on our way across the moors, to our end point of the day at Glaisdale Rigg.

After another pot of sweet tea, I reluctantly put some of my wet clothing back on, grabbed my bits and pieces and hobbled out of the pub and across the sharp stoned car park to the filming car, where I sat in the passenger seat with the heater on, blowing hot air into the footwell. I took advantage of this and threw all of my wet clothes down in the footwell to get as dry as they could before I headed back out on Day 12, part 2.

By now, the weather of the morning had completely gone, replaced by clear blue skies and hot sunshine. This day was a total tale of two halves weather wise, shitty morning and fantastic afternoon.

Pulling on my clothes, my signature "crazy hat", applying some Savlon to my wrecked feet and trying to rustle up the motivation, I got out of the film car and hobbled across the car park to meet Ian who was finishing getting ready for the afternoon ahead.

The contrast in weather from the morning made me feel so positive and ready to take on the afternoon/evening as we made our way across to Glaisdale Rigg.

We crossed the main road and waved to our support team as we headed off.

Having done this walk many times, I knew the grass on the side of the road would help me out, however, what I hadn't banked on was the main road had just been resurfaced a few days before with fresh road chippings. These road chippings had also covered the grass area at the side of the road as the new road surface was laid, and from the many cars using the road, kicking knife like chippings out into the grass verges.

Ian was way ahead of me at this point as I slowed down to a snail's pace whilst I tiptoed my way around the worst of the chippings. Looking ahead, it just appeared to be a nice grassy sidewalk, but every step contained the knife-like chippings. It was like this for just over a mile.

Rather than continue along the road to Rosedale Head and veer right at the junction, we opted to take the first right trail we came to, on the Esk Valley Walk, cutting off the corner and saving me from the immense pain of road chippings scratching at my feet as by now one of the big chippings made its way between my right big toe and the one next to it, slicing a vertical cut into it and it was bloody painful. It was like getting a paper cut between your toes and having that cut get battered with more chippings with each step taken and having no power to stop it.

Turning off onto the Esk Valley Walk, albeit for a short distance of about a kilometre, it allowed my feet to get a bit of a reprieve. This path was carved through the heath and contained a stone and dolomite type surface, which isn't ideal for anyone who is walking it barefoot, but it was a lot better than what I had just left behind on the main road.

Not long on this path, I could hear a buzzing noise getting closer. Ian had wandered off the path for a call of nature, and he came flying out of the heath at a rate of knots like a disturbed grouse. I burst out laughing as it was so funny to watch. A drone sent up by the guys filming the walk was making its way towards us at speed.

Luckily for Ian he heard it approaching from a distance away and took measures to make sure his integrity was still intact as the drone arrived overhead not long after he shot out of the heather.

Soon we were out of the heath and back onto the main road.

Leaving the Esk Valley Walk behind, we headed left onto Knott Road and walked along it for a kilometre and a half before we veered off onto a minor road that led us up Seavey Hill where we picked our trail up that would take us across Glaisdale Moor.

I have thought previous trails were the worst I had encountered on this adventure, before another appears on a different day that tops all the others. This new trail I had walked onto was now in the league of one of the most challenging I have had to undertake across the whole of the adventure.

It was challenging for Ian to walk and he had hiking boots on. For me, this became another point of the adventure challenge where I had to dig deep in my mind and fight the demons telling me I HAD to give up as it was impossible to complete barefoot and that the pain was too much.

They were right; the pain was too much; it was terrible. In fact, some of the worst pain I had experienced to date, BUT it wasn't impossible; There was heath to walk on and whilst it's not ideal, it would have to do. It would have to become my alternative path at the very worst bits on the main path.

Relying on heath however, had the adverse effect of damaging the tops of my feet more than they already were, as once again, like in previous times of walking on this "alternative" path, my feet would often disappear into the heather and on pulling them out to take the next step, the tops of the feet would come into contact with the brash root systems of the foliage, scratching the surface of the skin on the tops of my feet with each step, keeping the scabs from re-forming and creating new cuts.

Over the course of walking two kilometres on this horrible terrain my average speed had gone down from 1.8mph back at the road, to just half a mile an hour.

I needed to know how far I still had to go on this terrain as it was brutal so logged into the Garmin satellite tracker app that showed me exactly where we were. Thankfully, I had about a kilometre left to go before I hit a road again and it was then I noticed the place me and Ian were actually walking past at this very moment. It was a place on Glaisdale Moor identified on all mapping called "Cock Heads". Was this a sign? Was some higher power trying to tell us something here? What's the chances of 2 blokes walking this moor and me needing to check in and see where we were, only to be hit with "Cock Heads"?

Thankfully, prior to leaving the moor, the terrain became friendly again and with a spurt of energy, I mustered up the speed to get to the end of this nightmare trail.

With my feet at break point again and my ankles feeling like they had no more bend in them because of all the uneven terrain, we were soon off the moor and onto the road.

It was now 5.20pm and a lovely evening. It was warm, bright and being surrounded by moorland as far as the eye can see was just spectacular.

Normally 5.20pm would be too early to finish my daily miles as there was roughly around 5 hours of daylight left that I could use to my advantage, however the last few miles had took its toll on me both physically and mentally, and with bleeding feet, aching ankles and a broken mojo, I just needed to rest for a short while.

I sat in the sun with Ian discussing what we would love to eat right now as we munched on flapjacks. I fancied a huge steak, chips, onion rings and everything else piled on top. Ian was on the same page with steak or even a nice curry.

Dreaming over, we finished our "gourmet" flapjacks and as the skin on my feet was now beginning to tighten up, it was time to get a move on down the road.

Standing up and taking these first steps, even though only 10 minutes had elapsed since sitting down, it was difficult to get going again as my feet were literally seizing up.

For the next kilometre I walked on the road surface as it was smooth and helped my feet. It sounds strange but at this point even walking on grass was giving me pain as whilst the grass was quite cushioning; The ground was uneven and constantly twisting my already knackered ankles. At least the road was smooth and level.

The end of the walking day came quite sudden when my feet refused to work anymore. No matter how hard I tried to move them, the just weren't responding.

The juice in my feet had finally run out.

Ian came over and propped me up as I was at a place with myself where standing was proving to be difficult, and he knew that I couldn't make it to sit down on the grassy side of the road without help.

It was a tough day, one of the toughest so far given the morning weather, and terrain, and despite my end point coming earlier than expected, another 15 miles was now complete and in the bag!

Day 13

Glaisdale Rigg to Sneatonthorpe

Today was the day I had originally planned to finish my barefoot challenge, however having chased half a day loss of time because of the very challenging terrain to walk on around Ennerdale Water, taking 3 hours to do 1 mile at one point; falling down the side of the mountain and having to be rescued the same day, and then being advised to quit due to the trauma on my feet, I decided to add a day on to the challenge.

Quitting was not an option. I accepted that the other two things contributed to the impact on time, but I could never accept quitting.

I could have made it to Robin Hood's Bay today; However, it would have meant walking for 17 hours and I probably would have arrived at Robin Hood's Bay just before midnight.

Given there were many people planning to come and see me finish the challenge, some being kids, and it being a school night, it just made sense to add another day on to the adventure challenge. After all, my feet were in a terrible place and the thought of walking 16 hours on them just to hit my self-imposed deadline wasn't appealing at all.

After waking up and doing my daily meditation to clear my mind of any overnight negative thoughts, using this personal 10 minutes to align my goals and focus for the day ahead, I was up and doing my foot exercises, rocking ball to heel whilst the taught skin split and allowed the flexibility to return to my feet.

I knew from all the days gone by that I now needed an hour on a morning for my feet to work. Once again, the manuka foot cream and Savlon came into play to help make the skin on my feet more subtle and address the wounds to try to hold any infection at bay.

After a cup of coffee and a study of the map, the plan was to get to a point where tomorrow would be left in single figure miles, making for an easier day on the feet and to allow time for me and Ian to reflect on this journey, its highs and lows, the good and the bad, the laughs and the tears and what we have both learnt from our own personal experiences of this Coast to Coast challenge. Doing this also allowed for a safety buffer to ensure that if my feet were in a terrible way after today, I could still get to the finish line at all costs, something I would have done anyway, even if I had to crawl.

Continuing to exercise my feet, I was watching Ian putting his hiking boots on for the day ahead and I was so jealous. I was thinking how comfortable the boots must be feeling right now on his feet. It's true that you miss small things like this when you don't have them. We all take the small things in life for granted and only truly realise their worth when we don't have them in our life, just like what was happening right now.

Back home I have some really comfortable hiking boots and I was now imagining the feel of them on my feet, how they adapted to my walking style in the hills and how they kept my feet safe from the harshness of the mountains. Have I thought of these small little things when I put my hiking boots on in the past? Nope, I just took it all for granted.

The start of the day was perfect. Blue skies and warm rays from the sun lit up the whole expanse of Glaisdale Rigg and allowed us to see for miles. It's mornings like this that brought a feel-good factor in to play, offsetting the thoughts of having to walk across 13 miles of hills and moor.

The 2 holes in the bottom of my left foot had opened up once again meaning I had to start the day on the tarmac road and not the grass which was in abundance at the sides of the road. It was more painful walking on the grass, as the straw like base of each blade would stick right in the holes in my feet causing immense and sudden pain. Who would have thought grass could be your enemy when walking barefoot?

As we walked down the road, I noticed Ian quieter than usual and I figured he was having some quiet time thinking of home, his journey and the route ahead of us.

After a kilometre of walking down a relatively smooth road surface, it was time to veer right and onto a now familiar North Yorkshire Moors trail consisting of stone and a sandy dolomite type texture as we crossed over Glaisdale Moor and headed towards Glaisdale itself.

Prior to arriving at the main village centre, Ian found a "shortcut" on the map and figured it would save my feet a bit and shave off 10 minutes or so of the journey if we took it.

This sounded great to me, so I followed his every step. This path was a public footpath; However, it involved climbing over a stile and into a field full of cows.

Now, as you know from previous writings in this book, I am shit scared of cows and find them scary and unpredictable.

Despite beginning to panic at the thought of cows and my ability to not be able to run away from them if I needed to, because of having nothing on my feet, what happened next had me pissing myself as I climbed over the stile carefully. Ian was using his pole to clear the nettles for me and accidentally touched the electric fence with his other hand when he leaned on it. The noise he made, the unnatural body gestures he gave off that were out of his control, and the unrepeatable swear word combinations he made up was hilarious. I was crying with laughing.

The laughing soon stopped though as there must have been 20 cows in this field, all of who came over and take a look at these two strange looking humans now infiltrating their home.

Ian, like me, isn't a fan of cows and he walked fast towards the bottom corner of the field, leaving me to shit myself even more as the cows began to come closer in. I am of the belief of safety in numbers in situations like this, but Ian didn't share my view on this occasion and shot to the safety of the bottom corner after safely ducking under the electric fence.

I was taking slow careful steps through the field so as not to spook this big gang of cows, and every few feet I made towards safety, they would too. As I neared the bottom corner of the field, Ian used his walking pole to lift the electric fence and shouted "run." This was the wrong thing to do because as soon as I started legging it with my panic, so did the cows and it became a stampede towards me.

I dived under the electric fence, my heart pounding and my arse nipping.

The cows were all at the fence line, 3 layers deep and just standing there staring at me and Ian. There was literally a one-inch piece of electrified material separating us from this herd of killer cows.

It was one of the scariest moments I have experienced with cows.

Having nothing on my feet means I can't get myself out of danger as quickly as I usually would be able to, which leads to hesitation setting in whilst I weigh up the situation, and my reaction slows accordingly.

Soon I was back into a safe zone of village roads and following the road out of Glaisdale over the ford at Carr End, I was busted again!

Picking up the Esk Valley Walk, the official trail; I headed into East Arnecliffe Wood and needed a wee.

Ian walked ahead as I dipped off into a bushy area and shortly after, I heard an unnatural coughing from him which I thought strange. Next thing a dog was sniffing my ass, and I almost pissed on it. Trying to shoo it away with one hand was quite difficult, and I needed to get sorted quickly, as where there is a dog, there is normally an owner.

Popping out of the bushes and onto the path once again looked so weird as the dog's owner approached. I wasn't even going to justify it this time. I said "hi" and just walked on, trying to dodge the sharp bits of stone on the ground.

I wonder what the person thought when a bloke in a "crazy" hat, sunglasses and no shoes and socks on followed their dog out of the bushes? I have a feeling they may discuss the incident around their dinner table tonight.

After a kilometre of the woodland trail, which was fairly steady away under bare feet, I was soon back on the main road and heading towards Egton Bridge.

The road surface was bumpy in places but tolerable and as I walked the road, I once again noticed Ian go quiet and then start to get a bit antsy over little things happening. These signs began to take on a familiarity that I experienced on day eight of this adventure, which led to my full-on meltdown. Was Ian heading for one here?

In this world, they teach men not to show their true emotions and it is only of late where we have all been encouraged to talk about the darkness and things bothering us. In the past, people always perceived it as a weakness if men were to show their emotions, often leading to a pressure cooker effect that will inevitably blow one day.

By the time we arrived at Egton Bridge, the pressure cooker effect had caused Ian to blow in spectacular fashion. This was Ian's day for a meltdown.

We had stopped at the junction of Egton Manor and Ian was now saying he's not continuing on with the adventure, to which my reply was "yes you are, you have come this far, and you are not pulling out now". I knew this was the meltdown talking and not Ian as he too isn't a quitter in life.

As you have heard from my meltdown on day 8, little things are often magnified way bigger than their reality and having time to think about them can cause this pressure cooker effect. You are away from home, feeling low, feeling pain, pissed off with the weather, are tired, and many things, often experiencing them all at once and all it takes is something daft to happen that is completely out of your control at that moment in time and it is enough to trigger the full force of everything built up in you to this point, causing a blowout.

I'm not going to discuss the reasons for Ian's meltdown in this book, but needless to say something small that would normally be trivial and not bother Ian became an issue he felt out of control with at this point.

10 minutes later his meltdown was over, and Ian started laughing about it.

It is a hard thing to describe to anyone who hasn't experienced extreme situations that have prevailed for days and weeks, but it is very real.

After a big man hug, we discussed the next step of today's journey.

Our next stop would be Grosmont, a lovely little village that has a big railway heritage, with the railway still the dominant force of the village to this day, attracting visitors from all over the place wanting to experience the heritage services on the North Yorkshire Moors Railway.

Prior to setting off for Grosmont, a familiar face reappeared just like a genie popping out of the ground. It was Howy Soper, the guy who met me and Ian as we came across the North Yorkshire Moors near to Osmotherley. Being on another mid-week day off from work, he once again tracked my whereabouts via the satellite tracker and thought he would pop and say hello before heading off to Whitby. Howy is such a laid-back character in life who doesn't give a shit about most things and he lets nothing phase him.

Talking about characters, as I was chatting to Howy, a small white van pulled up having travelled the road I was about to walk down and a person who I can only describe as an absolute gentleman got out and asked to shake my hand.

He introduced himself as "Marrar of Egton Bridge". The name? He's everyone's Marrar, often written as Marra which is a northern word for a friend.

From Wiktionary, the definition of marra is: "marra (plural marras)

(West Cumbrian Predominantly, Geordie, Mackem) A friend, pal, buddy, mate.

Cheers marra!

Alreet marra?

How's it garn marra?"

I believe Marrar's real name is Tony Harland, a local farmer, but I'm sure nobody would probably know who he is if he started going by the name of Tony.

Marrar had been tracking my progress since he saw the news of my adventure on BBC1 almost a week ago and even had some people who worked for him doing the same and trying to locate me as I passed by the area, having them relay my position to him so he could drive and intercept me.

This man is one of the nicest people anyone could meet and who is definitely a larger-than-life character with his infectious banter. Marrar himself has raised many thousands of pounds for charities and causes close to his heart and for that I salute him.

Being in his late seventies, he puts many a younger person to shame with the graft he does and the hours he packs into each day.

Adventuring for me doesn't just create good memories; it also allows me to meet some amazing people and this Coast to Coast adventure has been full of them.

Leaving Marrar and Howy behind, it was time for me and Ian to make our way to Grosmont.

The path from Egton Manor and past the Sewage Works was tough going, with my average mph dropping again to less than a mile an hour as I navigated my way along the challenging terrain. Marrar had warned me of this path, however there was nothing I could do about it, I needed to walk along it, so I just made the best of the situation and cracked on.

Waiting at the other end of this path was my support team with water top ups, and it was a welcome sight to see the lads.

After taking five minutes and having some banter with the lads, a car pulled up, a familiar face jumped out, stuffed chocolate and water in mine and Ian's hands, waved bye and drove off. You guessed it; it was Howy... AGAIN, just doing his bit to help.

The generosity of people helping in small ways, most of whom have been complete strangers, has been phenomenal on this adventure.

The walk into Grosmont forced me onto the paths as the roads became busy with vehicles. The faces of drivers and passengers in the vehicles as they passed me was so funny to watch. People looked, looked away and looked back again with long stares as if to say to themselves "Have I really just seen a guy in a funny hat with no shoes and socks on?"

People walking down the street towards me acted in a not too dissimilar way. Behaviour from folk in this little village was ranging from people blatantly staring at me, some people pretending they never saw me and even one couple who crossed over the road to just get out of my way.

Coming into Grosmont I noticed two St John Ambulances parked up near to the public toilets on Front Street so I wandered over and asked the medics if they had anything I could put on my feet to help draw out the ingrained stone and dirt in the cuts and to help me get rid of the green puss coming from one of my toes on my right foot.

They were astounded that I had come all the way from St Bees and was actually still standing and able to walk, however they were concerned at the same time at the state of my feet.

One lady looked at my feet, disappeared into the back of one ambulance, and reappeared with some antiseptic wipes. I said given the pain level when my feet are touched at the moment, I would rather do the wiping. She gave me enough wipes to fill part of my bum-bag (fanny pack to my American friends reading this), gathered everyone from St John together for a group photo with the "crazy" hat man and then I was back off on my travels once again.

The last time I had been anywhere near to Grosmont was when I was a kid, so I had forgotten about the "one road in and a very steep road" out of the place. When I say steep, it's a 33% gradient meaning I would have to put a lot of weight onto my feet as I headed up and onto Black Brow and the moorland ahead. Thankfully, once on Fair Head Lane, I could alternate from road to grass, depending on how it was on my feet.

Grass would normally be the answer and my quick win, however the holes in my left foot had once again become problematic so depending on the type of grass on the sides of the road (I didn't realise how many types of grass there are), it was often easier and less painful to walk on the tarmac as it avoided the sharp stems of the grass sticking directly into the holes in my foot causing pure discomfort and pain.

Once at the gateway to the open moor it was time for a pit stop to rest my feet and have some food.

Laid on the grass enjoying the sun, it was hard to think that tomorrow would be the very last day of doing all of this.

With 5 miles still ahead of me that incorporated a good bit of technical terrain for a barefoot guy to take on, I finished my pie, dusted myself down and hit the road... literally, as the grass was making things uncomfortable for my left foot.

After heading off the moor I was Intercepted by Paul Burgum, a friend and a big influence on my extreme adventures. Paul has an amazing life story whereby he has conquered and overcome so many things to become the person he is today. I highly recommend his book "Jumping the cliff to simply be" as it is so inspiring to read.

Jumping out of his car, Paul ran over and gave me a big man hug, something that meant a lot to me. He knew I was quite broken with this adventure and his words of encouragement went a long way.

Paul had his young son and his dog with him, so he parked his car up way ahead and the next thing I saw was a figure running towards me with his son in a backpack chair and dog in tow. It was true Paul style and as extreme as it comes. Paul helped motivate me as he walked alongside me and stayed with me till we got to the B1416 road where me and Ian needed to cross and head out on a trail to get to Sneatonthorpe.

After exchanging another man hug and telling Paul I would see him in a short while, me and Ian were over a stile and instantly battling nettles of all heights and types.

Ian was using his hiking pole like a light sabre, chopping a path through them to try to make things easy under foot for me. It didn't help the fact I was in shorts and it wasn't long before my legs began to feel the wraith of the nettles.

Breaking out of this confined mini copse into open fields brought a reprieve from the nettles and helped me gain some lost pace. It wasn't long though before we found ourselves surrounded in the "hole of hell" with thistles and wheat intertwined in a field which we needed to be through, or at least thought we needed to be.

These thistles were chest high and there was no way of avoiding them. Every step taken at this point was horrible. The thistles were so intertwined with wheat that it was impossible to flatten them. It was another case of "it is what it is" shoulder the pain and just carry on.

Halfway through this field, Ian checked the map and realised we had come too far and missed our right-hand turn back onto the trail. "You are shitting me?" I replied, feeling so disillusioned at this.

We were so focussed on dealing with the thistles, which incidentally were also beginning to give Ian a great deal of discomfort, that we made the classic mistake of focussing our energies on that one task and missed checking the map at a crucial point.

All was not lost though. It just meant we had to double back through the field till we found the point to access the trail again, which ironically was covered in chest high thistles and nettles; possibly one of the reasons we missed it in the first place.

By now my feet were numb with the stinging pain which happened by having no option but to retrace our steps and walk on the now semi flattened thistles, along with the discomfort of the blebs covering my legs formed from the nettle and thistle, however, given there was nothing I could do about the situation I just sucked it up and stayed quiet.

Popping out of the fields at Sneatonthorpe to meet back up with Paul Burgum, who by now had driven round to our location, I noticed a couple of locals milling around, inquisitive at what was going on in their tiny village today.

Whilst I am sure the locals are used to hikers passing by their homes daily, I guess someone wandering past in bare feet was something worth coming out of their houses to witness for real on this occasion.

Paul B had a look at my feet whilst I was sorting them out and rubbing a doc leaf on them, trying to rid them of the stinging sensation after the butchering they just took from the nettle and thistle infested fields I had just walked through, and he was surprised at the thickness of skin I had gained over the course of 13 months of training for my barefoot adventure. The skin on the balls of my feet and heels had a good quarter of a centimetre of hard skin on them which reduced the visible trauma from the adventure, however the places where the skin was a lot thinner, such as the arch of my feet, under the toes and of course on the tops of my feet all bore the trauma of the adventure.

Despite thicker skin round the main points of contact on my feet, it didn't lessen the pain any. It just meant my feet withstood more of a battering around these tougher parts before the skin started to become damaged.

After spending 10 minutes having banter with Paul Burgum and the obligatory adventurer pics together, it was time to bag the last kilometre of the day.

Following the road past Rigg Farm, one of the locals I spoke to earlier caught up with me in her car and idled along next to me and chatted through her open window, keeping me company and my mind active for this last push of the day.

The aim was to get to the end of this road before it went off to the right and call this the end point of the day, leaving only 6 miles in total to complete on the adventure tomorrow, allowing me and Ian some much-needed reflection time, be able to take our time to chat and take in the coastal views without the urgency to press on and finish the day.

Day 14

Sneatonthorpe to Robin Hoods Bay

Finishing yesterday's segment a stone's throw away from the east coast and leaving a single figure mileage for the day ahead, I stayed in Whitby overnight and I felt so refreshed after a decent night's sleep. I must have literally passed out when my head hit the pillow.

Being the day the challenge comes to a close, and with only 6 miles to complete, there was no urgency to get going on the trail like there has been for the previous 13 days of this adventure.

My feet were in need of their morning exercises and I craved caffeine to kick my head and ass into gear.

Throughout the adventure challenge there has been a lot of media interest and at 7.15am I was due another call with my friends at the BBC to discuss my last day of the challenge, my thoughts, and to once again recap the last 13 days.

My interview with Paul Addison and Amy Oakden from BBC Tees was so upbeat and we had such a lively chat about my adventure, my feet, and even the colour of my toenail varnish. These folks are FAB, and the Beeb have been so supportive of this adventure challenge. The interview really put my mind in a positive place from the outset and created a "feel-good factor."

After the interview I thought I'd sneak into Ian's room and ambush him while he slept, just for the comedy value as he is so funny when he kicks off.

When I got to his room there was no sign of him, where was he at this early time of day? Just as I was turning to leave his room he jumped out from the far side of his bed and made a roar like a tiger, frightening the living shit out of me in the process. I guess you can't kid a kidder as the old saying goes, and he obviously had the same idea as me. I'm just glad he didn't do it to me when I was live on the radio; that would have made interesting listening if he had tried to set me up.

After another coffee and more feet exercising, I began to get my gear on for the day ahead. It was a sunny day; The sunbeams were dancing through the window and scattering across the floor. A quick check on my weather app for the day ahead helped me decide on the layers, coat, etc I needed to take with me.

Given there was only 6 miles to complete today on what was predicted to be decent pathways, it allowed me to run through things I needed to get ready for the day, study the route on the map, check I had packed the satellite tracker, the external power supply and the charging lead for my phone, should I need to fall back on it.

Today was so laid back compared to every other morning start of the past 14 days. These past days were a rush to get on the trail to make use of as much daylight as I could, not even giving my feet the right amount of time they needed to warm up.

To be able to sit round a table, having a laugh with Ian and the lads and just taking the piss out of life itself without the rush was such a blessing. It's rare that it happens like this on an adventure.

On prior adventures they have been as brutal as stopping at a random point, getting an hour or so sleep, getting back up, shaking the sleep off and just cracking straight back on with things in an almost robotic way to ensure the miles for the day are packed in and complete, and sometimes like this for months at a time.

Today would be so different.

Throughout this barefoot journey across the country, it has been a constant battle with the terrain, the elements, my mind, the physical pain, along with not getting the chance to take in the beauty of my surroundings as I transited through some spectacular places in the 3 National Parks that the Coast to Coast takes you through.

The plan from the outset when I lengthened the adventure by a day was to use this last day to reflect with Ian on our personal experiences of the adventure, our difficulties over the previous 13 days, chat about the highs and lows and prepare our minds for our end point of Robin Hood's bay.

We could do this in a stop start way with no rush as we couldn't be in Robin Hood's Bay till 7pm where a small welcoming reception was waiting for us from one of my Charities, the Chris Lucas Trust. I also knew kids were coming for 7pm from a local Hartlepool charity that helps to nurture people's creativity, a group called Creative Minds.

Today is so different to other days gone by. It's a first that we would arrive at our endpoint way before an agreed time if we weren't careful, meaning we had to quite literally slow things down to get there at the agreed time. Every other day so far has been a battle just to get to an end point before the daylight was lost or my feet completely gave up on me.

Picking up where we left off from the night before on Mill Lane, it was now 9.15am and we had a glorious day ahead of us.

Heading along the road, I found the surface aggravating my feet more than it did yesterday. It was the same road, same road surface, so why was it being an issue today?

It then became clear that when setting off from the gravelly pull-in point at the bend of the road, I must have stood in some small fragments of glass without realising it before heading off for the day. Under normal circumstances, standing in these small shards of glass would have been picked up right away with the pain they would bring, however because of the numbness in the soles of my feet I didn't even realise they were there until I was walking on them.

After a quick pit stop to dust the soles of my feet down and pull out any embedded slivers of glass that had made their way into the soles of my feet, I was soon back on the road again.

Taking a right onto Back Lane, we were soon passing through Low Hawsker and then crossing the A171 road into the small village of High Hawsker.

High Hawsker was a significant place to pass through as on the map it meant we were only a kilometre from the coastal path and soon the route would bring seaside views from the cliffs as Robin Hood's Bay got closer with each step.

The route took us through Northcliffe Holiday Park before intercepting the coastal path at the cliff's edge. Just as I was walking into the holiday park, two ladies stopped me and began chatting away like we were lifelong friends. They had been out for a jog, saw the crazy hat and popped over to say hi and wish me all the best for the last push of the adventure. Their kind words brought a lump to my throat.

Walking through the holiday park brought with it a few stares from people sitting on the verandas of their caravans, enjoying a morning cuppa in the sunshine. I wonder what they were thinking.

It wasn't long before we hit the coastal path and it was time to take a pit stop and kill some time, otherwise we would be in Robin Hood's Bay within a couple of hours, way ahead of our agreed time.

This was the perfect time to chill out in the sunshine and take stock of the journey so far. Up till now, both me and Ian have never had time to reflect on anything let alone talk openly about our personal experiences.

I have known Ian since the 90s and have been through a lot with him when we served in Search and Rescue, and in our personal lives as best friends; However, it has taken this adventure to really get to know him, what made him tick and what made him human.

Do I see Ian any differently now this adventure is pretty much over? I do, and for the better. I see a person who's persona is hard as hell on the outside, yet underneath he is very human and sensitive to the things everyone else is. For years he has hidden this well, but then again, that is what us fellas are good at; hiding the emotion.

I figured now was a good time to do a video update for my social media followers, and the response to it was amazing. The encouragement flooded through for both me and Ian, and the messages of support were overwhelming.

Continuing round the coastal path, I was intercepted by Terry Ridley who had walked up from Robin Hood's Bay, tracking my progress. Terry had made the journey down from Redcar to see me finish and had decided to walk up onto the cliff path and meet up with me and walk for a while.

So far, the coastal path had been great on my feet as it comprised dry mud and grass with the odd stone and boulder here and there.

Interestingly, at points on the path a blue nylon rope disappeared over the edge of the cliff and when I tried to figure out where it went it made me feel queasy as getting close to the edge always made me nervous, knowing the erosion of the cliff edges could make it crumble and disappear without notice.

I'd gone over the edge once on this adventure, back on day two, and didn't fancy it a second time so retreated to the safety of the path.

A few more people stopped me on the coastal path as they had heard I was in the area and after a few selfies it was time for the final push.

Throughout the day I had made a conscious effort not to break my feet; I was literally walking and scanning the coastal path constantly to avoid all kinds of sharp things as it would have totally pissed me off if an injury put me out of the game at the last few miles of the adventure, given all I had gone through both physically and mentally over the last 2 weeks to get to this point.

As I came out of the field and began to enter the top end of Robin Hood's Bay, I started wondering if many people other than the charity and Creative Minds would be at the finish line?

I have met a lot of great people on this journey, most of whom had already finished the Coast to Coast a day or so before me. A few more people passed me today and said they would see me at the finish line for a well-earned pint.

I was beginning to feel nervous, anxious and excited at the same time for what lay ahead. The end point was finally here. I had worked up to this point for the last 2 weeks.

The reality was I was so glad to be completing this adventure so the pain in my feet and mind would finally stop. For days I had kept everything at bay but each day it was becoming harder to keep pushing the pain back and stopping the darkness from swamping me

Approaching 7pm and coming into Robin Hoods Bay via the top car park, the sun was shining, and it was a great evening. Robin Hood's Bay was so busy for this time of day.

As I was preparing to make the steep walk down to the bottom of the bank and to the official end point of the Coast to Coast, people began stopping me and congratulating me on my efforts, and whilst walking down the steep bank with Ian, I saw both sides of the road begin to line up with people who came out to see us finish... is this really happening? Have I really captured the imagination of people that much with this adventure?

Despite having many adventures under my belt and experiencing the finish of them, my feelings for this particular adventure ending was a mixed bag of emotions.

It was so tough to complete on one hand, and the end point couldn't come soon enough, yet on the other hand I felt I would miss the daily grind of it and no longer being immersed in the countryside.

Walking down the steep road, Ian shed some tears behind his sunglasses as the emotion of finishing the challenge and seeing his family got the better of him and I remember thinking to myself "I am proud to have shared this adventure with him and how I may not have even been here today had it not been for him coming down the side of that mountain and saving my ass on day two". For this, I will be forever grateful to Ian.

As we neared the bottom of the bank, Ian's grandkids Jack and Noah came up to greet us and walked the rest of the way down with us. People began clapping as we walked by, shaking our hands and the sound of singing over a loudspeaker system was becoming more prominent.

As we turned the tight last corner to come out into the open area at the bottom of the bank, we could see a huge crowd of people who had gathered, the kids from Creative Minds singing songs to welcome us back and there was such a great buzz going on.

Any pain at this point had now vanished! The mind is a powerful thing, isn't it?

We had to initially walk past everyone who came out to see us so we could dip our feet in the sea on the bottom slipway. I dipped my feet in and yelped at the saltwater stinging my wounds whilst Ian went one step further and just dived in as the tide was high.

There were big hugs all round, and I made a beeline to see my good friend and head of the Chris Lucas Trust, Lynn Lucas. Lynn, her husband Lynn, Sharon and Steph saw me off at the start and they were back again to see me at the finish. I love these guys!

There were so many faces I was noticing in the crowd and needed to get round and see them, but before anything, I headed over to the Bay Horse Hotel with Ian to sit under the plaque on the side of the wall that signified "The End" of the Coast to Coast and to capture the moment with a picture.

Walking back over to chat with people, a complete stranger thrust a pint in my hand, said well done and disappeared! Thanks! That pint was so welcomed, and it went down a treat.

People I had walked with over the last couple of weeks were at the end point, as were a couple of my Gym family members who travelled down to see me finish, canny strangers who were bewildered at all that was going on shook mine and Ian's hands, Ian's family too had travelled down to see us and the amazing Creative Minds were there in force.

Singing a Robbie Williams rendition and absolutely nailing it was little Charlie Atchinson. Charlie is six years old and has an amazing talent that is being nurtured from the team at Creative Minds.

Despite his young age, Charlie has been out singing in places such as Liverpool, Durham and around the North-East region helping to raise funds towards the Chris Lucas Trust and now he is here welcoming me back with some songs.

Creative Minds have really done me proud with the banners they have put up, the makeshift stage they set up for all their young artists to perform for everyone who has turned out to see me and Ian return, and for their help in raising more money at the finish event for great causes.

This really was an emotional end to a very tough couple of weeks.

After around 40 minutes of hanging out with everyone who had turned up to see us, it was time to head off. We were bundled into the support car and whisked off to Whitby for the evening. I'm so pleased the support team were there with the car as it meant I didn't have to climb the steep bank in bare feet to meet them there.

The Aftermath

After the surreal reception I experienced on my arrival at Robin Hood's Bay on Friday the 21st June, after 14 days of crossing the country completely barefoot, I was bundled into a car with Ian and headed up the coast to Whitby for the evening.

I envisaged this would be a long night of alcohol and laughs, finished with a calorie packed stinky kebab.

Throughout the whole adventure, I had a rolled-up pair of jeans and t-shirt packed safely in a dry bag in the bottom of my backpack for this very night. It served as a mental reminder that there will be an endpoint to this adventure. I used the touch of the dry bag at points when the going was tough as a mechanism to re-focus my mind and have it serve as a positive anchor point. "It may be tough going now but think of the party at the end of it" I kept saying to myself.

Half an hour later I was in Whitby, and the car travel alone was sufficient for the skin on my swollen, scabbed feet to tighten up. I rode the whole way with my head on the rear passenger window as I was exhausted and just wanted to sleep. The more I thought about sleep, the more it kept me awake. Funny how that happens isn't it? It's like hearing a dripping tap. The more you try not to hear it; the louder it becomes.

Getting out of the car in Whitby was no mean feat (or feet ha). I had stiffened up and wasn't feeling the best.

My head was banging from the vibration off the car's window and the second I moved my feet to shuffle out of the rear seat in the car, they split open again and I could feel the skin just tearing like paper.

I was sore, very sore. My feet were dirty, ingrained and had stones embedded in the open wounds. I still had my backpack on and had travelled half an hour without even realising it. That explains why I found it tough to put the rear seat belt on. I thought I was just getting fatter than usual.

Ian grabbed hold of me to steady me on my feet as I walked the short distance to the house. I really wasn't in a good place with it. It was as if my mind was saying "you've done it... challenge complete, now I'm shutting your body down for a while."

The climb up the stairs was challenging, despite it being carpeted and feeling amazing under foot, as I made my way to the bathroom to sort a much-needed bath out.

I had to use the stair rail to literally pull myself up. Each stair walked was achieved by putting one foot on it, pull myself up and then get the other foot on the same stair, and then repeat.

Standing in the bathroom and looking at myself in the mirror, I looked a wreck. Unshaven for two weeks, stinky, clothes all dirty, face covered in grime, crazy hat still in place and backpack still on my back; I needed someone just to come in and get a grip of me and help me out.

My feet now felt like they were going through a phase of heating up. They were radiating immense pain and felt like they were now on fire. I didn't want to look at them as I knew they were in a bad place.

After unclipping the backpack and just letting it hit the floor, I sat on the toilet seat and put my head in my hands and thought to myself, "what have I done?"

Should I be happy that I've just crossed the country through some of the worst June weather ever and taken on some of the most challenging terrain completely barefoot? If I was, I wasn't feeling it right now

This was a "behind closed door moment" that I didn't want anyone to see. I had to figure this feeling out in my mind and get my feet working again. I felt like the world had just closed in on me and I was looking through a tunnel at my situation.

This wasn't good, and I needed to kick myself up the ass and keep these demons at bay.

The pain was intensifying to a point where I could literally feel my pulse radiating through my feet with every heartbeat and coursing through the rest of my body. It was like a stone thrown in a pond (my feet) and the ripples radiating out (the rest of my body), every time my heart did a beat.

I couldn't take any painkillers as I was going out with my support team and friends from Whitby and there was no way I was mixing alcohol and painkillers. It was a case of "suck it up buttercup" and get in the bloody bath!

Sinking my feet in a hot bath should have been bliss, however it was anything but fun!

It was at this point that I was sick! Physically sick over the side of the bath. Thankfully, the lack of food in my stomach didn't make too much of a mess.

Normally at the end of an adventure or even a day in the mountains, the appeal of a long steep in a hot bath is a real motivator. Right now, though, I wanted to be out of this bath pronto.

I had to address the stones and grime in the open wounds on my feet and try to get them out in the most pain-free way as I could or there would be no way I could go out around Whitby for the evening.

I had shoes dropped off at the house prior to my challenge finishing and trying to put socks on over open wounds and then stuff my feet into a pair of shoes was very difficult. Firstly, the shoes no longer fitted me. A few weeks before my brogues were a great fit, however with all the swelling and trauma, I could barely stuff my feet into them. I needed to get my feet in them though, as firstly no pub would allow me in without footwear on, and secondly, the thought of walking around barefoot after what I had been through, and when I no longer needed to was a no go.

I even contemplated asking Dan if I could borrow a pair of his shoes as he was two sizes bigger than me, but given the state of my feet, I knew what his answer would have been.

Despite it being a lovely evening with the sun shining and no breeze, I was shivering. It was the post challenge "come down" I was experiencing. I have experienced this many times before and the feeling is as if your body is going into shock. First your teeth start chattering and next your body begins shaking, sometimes uncontrollably.

The only coat I had in Whitby other than my smelly adventure coat was my down-filled jacket. It wasn't ideal, and I was sure to get the stares in pubs given it was a lovely summer's evening and I was wearing an insulated jacket, but I didn't care at this point.

It was good to be out having a beer with those close to me and some of whom had supported me on this adventure, but I felt like a bit of a party pooper. I was having to sit down a lot as my feet couldn't take the "standing in one place" thing we all do on a night out. Despite this, it was a cracking evening, and everyone ended up getting very drunk.

By now, Ian was singing into his imaginary microphone and passing it over to me to sing along to as well while the guy on the small stage area in the George Hotel was belting out his cover of "The Devil went down to Georgia".

What a great way to shut down an extreme couple of weeks.

Saturday morning came around, and get this, my first day post challenge started hangover free!

I couldn't believe it after all the beer I had drank with the lads the night before which was just as well, as I had a scheduled interview at 8.10am on BBC Tees with Scott Makin about the challenge, so I needed to sound my best. Scott is a great interviewer, and we had some good banter on the wireless.

Not long after, I was in the passenger seat of the car and on my way home!

On arriving back in Hartlepool an hour later, I let myself into the house and was met with a possessed ultra-dog bouncing all over me. For a little dog, she was bouncing around and trying to climb inside me. I guessed she missed me whilst I had been away.

Having brought all my kit indoors after it was dumped with me on my lawn, I sat with the kids who had made me a big welcome home banner and gave me my belated Father's Day cards.

I could feel the emotion building up inside of me before I even opened them, but I was determined not to cry. I had to show the kids I was a tough adventurer! It was no good though; I broke down reading their cards. I was in floods of tears.

I could see Jayden, my son, staring at my feet and then turning away, then he did it again, and again, trying to process these images.

I knew my feet weren't in good health, however looking down at them to see what was making the boy look, then look away and so on, I noticed my feet had turned purple. I'm no doctor, however, this wasn't right, that I knew for sure.

After a bit of persuasion by Jo, I headed off to Urgent Care at the University Hospital of Hartlepool and hobbled barefoot through the doors to the reception area.

After a short wait, they ushered me into a room where a male nurse and his student were waiting to see me.

After telling the nurse the story behind my horrible feet, his reaction was priceless. He was in awe, but at the same time concerned for my wellbeing. They would try to remove the crap from the wounds by washing them in some sort of potion, however I asked them not to because of the pain I was experiencing and that I would do that bit myself at home.

Given they now deemed me high risk as I had been walking barefoot through farmyard slurry with open wounds, through cow shit and places that carry a high risk of disease, I braced myself for what was to follow.

Not only was I prescribed a course of some of the strongest antibiotics available, I had to have a tetanus injection in my left arm and a diphtheria injection in my right arm.

I might be covered in tattoo's, but truth be known, I don't like needles.

I was dreading this!

Lucky for me, my feet were creating so much pain, and thankfully this nurse was a bit of a wizard with injections, I never felt a thing in either arm as the needles were stuck in.

Armed with a prescription of Naproxen painkillers, paracetamol and stuff to stop the naproxen causing stomach issues due to its side effects, I was off home and spent the rest of the day sat on my backside with my feet in a bowl of cold water, trying to stop them from banging.

After a restless night with the throbbing in my feet, I eventually got up at 20 past 10...WTF??? I never sleep beyond 5.30am normally. This is probably the latest I have ever got out of bed in my life.

I took a day out of life and laid in bed watching TV and shovelling the meds down my throat, but not long after this, the boredom kicked in.

Those who know me know I am not a person for sitting down and doing nothing with my life. I have to be doing something as life is too short to let days pass by. Right now though, my feet were forcing me to do nothing... I wasn't a happy bunny!

By 3.30pm I'd had enough of the boredom, so I strapped my feet up, squeezed into a pair of plimsols and went to see Ian for a coffee and a bit of post challenge banter. Even though it was only a day and a half since we had last seen each other, I missed the "lad banter" from us both.

To date, my feet are still having issues.

For more than a month after I finished my challenge I was woken up during the night with a pulsing pain in the soles of my feet and more weirdly an itch going from the sole of my right foot, travelling internally to my knee. The inside of my foot was so itchy, but I couldn't scratch it and it drove me mad as the itch was deep inside!

Things just weren't improving, so I arranged an appointment with the doctor and after seeing the nurse practitioner, I was given another 60 days of painkillers to combat the constant throbbing I was experiencing.

Over time, my feet have returned to normal. There is still a way to go and I am falling back on the painkillers when things get too bad, however I am now into a training routine and preparing for my next big adventure challenge. I am building this training up slowly, being more mindful of my feet and how they are an important feature on my body and having taken my feet for granted throughout my life, I appreciate them now more than ever.

Barefoot Earthing / Grounding

'Connecting us and the Planet'

Over the last few years, there has been a lot of research and studies conducted that lead to the belief that by connecting to the planets natural energy system through walking barefoot on grass, dirt, sand, stone or rock, it can massively reduce the onset of pain, tiredness and other ailments that burden so many people in this day and age.

This connection with the earth is often referred to as 'Grounding' or 'Earthing'

These studies concluded that when your bare feet come into direct contact with the earth, an exchange of electrons takes place, and this exchange transfers these electrons from the ground and into the human body and that the absorption of these electrons help to neutralise free radicals that can often lead to inflammation, disease and other issues.

The planet is a natural conductor of electrons and so are all living things, including us mere mortals. Given our bodies comprise of water and minerals, it means we are naturally great conductors of electricity which aids us by grounding us with the planet.

Energy received directly from the earth has been shown to enhance your body and contributes to an overall positive wellbeing by improving vitality and allowing for a more restful and natural sleep. It also puts the body into a state of harmony and helps to maintain the body's biological rhythms, vastly reduces and even eradicates inflammation, making it one of the most natural and powerful anti-inflammatory and anti-aging remedies out there today! It is in abundance around us, is free, and you will really enjoy connecting with the planet and earthing yourself!

Advances in technology have created a "modern" fast paced way of living for most of us, however it is vital we maintain a connection to the planet and nature around us. Our change in lifestyles over the years has seen many of us become disconnected from our bond with the surrounding earth.

Since the dawn of civilisation, human beings have walked the earth, farmed their lands with bare hands (and feet), sat, ate and slept on the ground, naturally grounding themselves. In this modern day, however, we have become increasingly disconnected from nature by our modern, fast-paced lifestyle. We have replaced the footwear of old with heavily insulated rubber and plastic soled shoes, breaking our connection to the earth as these materials are no longer allowing conductivity to naturally flow.

Our modern lifestyle has blocked us from our natural connection to the earth. we are now conducting life "off the ground", insulated by plastic, tarmac, carpets etc as these are all a main part of our life, surrounding us everywhere and they act as a block to our natural connection with the earth. We are constantly bombarded with radiation from objects and appliances that have become part of our daily existence. WiFi, mobile phones, microwaves, smart speakers, TV's and other household devices, with reports suggesting damage being caused to our bodies.

Grounding / Earthing helps to reduce these harmful radicals by using the earth's energy to help naturally repair cells and tissue that can get damaged along the way.

Connecting with the natural abundance of energy via Grounding / Earthing is a very effective way to remain in good health and reduce damaging effects of our modern, fast-paced lives.

For me, the effects of earthing have been very noticeable. Once over the initial and very weird feeling under foot (something that happens to us all the first time we experience barefoot walking), one of the biggest things I experienced was clarity of mind.

I have a continually active mind given the life I lead, and in the past, I have often found it hard to switch things off, causing me to overthink things and turn something small into something that takes over my head.

Barefoot walking helped clear my mind of negatives and things I couldn't put right immediately, allowed me to enjoy the space around me and helped me forward plan the positive things in life, and set goals.

The audible experience was enhanced for me too. Prior to barefoot walking, a trip in the countryside was a pretty standard thing to do for me, having done it all my life, so the sounds of nature became just another one of those things and something I didn't really take advantage of and appreciate.

Barefoot walking seemed to enhance my senses, allowing me to hear nature with more clarity, helped me smell the country air around me and feel connected to our world.

One of the most noticeable things barefoot wandering helped me overcome was an injury picked up back in 2017 after a 10,000-mile adventure. This daily pounding on my knees for 336 days caused my left knee to get thrown out, inducing great pain and discomfort. Diagnoses ranged from stress fractures (shin splints) to anterior knee pain syndrome, patellofemoral malalignment, chondromalacia patella, and iliotibial band syndrome. A lot of fancy words for something that caused discomfort.

After visits to the physio with little effect, a combination of rehab in the gym for strengthening the muscle wastage that was happening, along with barefoot grounding saw my knee return to health.

I run with a weird gait, meaning I run on the outer sides of my feet, causing the knee to take some stress it shouldn't. After a prolonged time of doing this, the resulting injury was inevitable. Gait was something I was not even aware of back in 2017, so I just pressed on.

Gait is the way you walk, step, run etc and apparently mine is deemed as under-pronation. I'm not alone with this type of gait with a good portion of the population under pronating in their running style.

As the foot strikes the floor, it hits the ground at a steeper than normal angle, causing a jarring effect, causing shock through the lower leg.

At the time I was always wondering why I was burning out running footwear at a rate of knots on the outer edges... I was expecting decent running shoes to last 500 miles, but I was changing them every 300 miles due to the way I was running.

Barefoot walking and running helps you straighten your stance. I found that trying to walk or run barefoot the same way I did with running shoes on just didn't work. It was also very painful!

For a start, my feet now contact the floor with the balls first, hitting the ground in more of a flatter way, than on the edges, plus striking the ground hard and first with my heel was now no longer happening. Walking barefoot corrected everything about the way I have always walked the earth.

Whether it's coincidence or because of the grounding effect barefoot walking has on our bodies, I have not suffered from a cold in a year and a half and my focus on tasks at hand are a lot sharper, holding my concentration for longer.

As I have mentioned above, there have been a plethora of studies undertaken in the benefits of barefoot walking and running, grounding ourselves to this wonderful planet.

If you are interested in trying it or for more information on the benefits to be had from walking barefoot and grounding yourself, visit www.earthinginstitute.net.

Final Thoughts

Believe in yourself and you will achieve great things in this life. My Barefoot adventure was definitely the toughest thing I have ever undertaken in my life, however, from the outset of this extreme challenge I had this unfaltering belief in myself that I would complete it no matter what.

As you have read in this book, there has been many times when the going was so tough that no one would have blamed me if I had quit, but this was never an option for me.

I had the belief in myself, had the end goal figured out for what I wanted to achieve, and I just had to deal with the bits that happened in between the start and finish of my adventure.

Despite this, it was tough, very tough in fact and by the end of the adventure challenge, I really thought I had been To Hell and Back - BAREFOOT.

I have this inbuilt ability to think of something in life that I want to complete, figure a plan out for it and see the successful end result. By seeing and visualising the event completed BEFORE I even do it, it helps condition my mind to accept it WILL be a success.

Believing in yourself is an absolute must.

I began this story by letting you all into my life from when I was told I would turn out to be a failure because I wasn't prepared to follow the crowd, in this case, my dad wanting me to follow him into his work, the done thing for most kids leaving school back in the day.

I didn't believe for a minute I would be a failure and used the power of this verbal negativity to breed success in my life. I wasn't prepared to accept anything but success. My dad gave me the best gift ever, and he didn't even realise it at the time. To this day, he eats his words.

All you have to remember is a belief is a feeling of absolute certainty. If you want to achieve anything in life, you need to be certain in your mind that you will achieve it.

You must believe in yourself completely. This is something I did long before I started the barefoot challenge.

Our beliefs control our results because we will never take action towards something that we don't believe is possible. Had I had even the slightest doubt that this adventure would be anything but successful, this would have been the single negative crack it needed that would have probably spread as the days wore on, almost guaranteeing my failure.

Here's the thing, you can achieve ANYTHING you set your mind to if you have that belief in yourself.

You can be the most educated person in the world, expecting the world to fall at your feet, but if you don't have the belief in what you want to achieve, it doesn't matter one bit. If you don't believe you can do it, you will never achieve it.

Belief in yourself is so important and combining this with setting your sights on your end goal it becomes a dynamic combination for success.

The reality is that most people don't achieve what they want in life. It's not because they aren't capable or lack the opportunity to achieve; It's because most people really don't know what they want.

You heard me right. Most people don't know what they want in this life and just wander along, going with the flow. Imagine if they knew what they wanted, believed they could get it and set themselves a goal of getting it. Boosh! It's a game changer.

The stark reality is that only 3% of people set goals in this life.

It's worth mentioning at this point not to confuse a goal with a wish.

How often have you wished you had something, but the wish never came true? You wish you had that flash car but no matter how hard you wished; the car just never materialised. You are in effect, daydreaming at this point.

Setting a goal, however, to get that car, and believing in yourself to achieve that goal, brings around a whole new way of getting what you want because you are changing your mindset.

Your goal is the car and you will do what it takes to achieve your goal, as opposed to sitting there, looking up at the sky and wishing a divine intervention would happen for you.

Set goals that excite you and push you beyond your limits. If your goals are all too easy to achieve, they need to be upped because they are not big enough.

Many people avoid taking action towards their goals as they feel they're not ready and need more time to build up their confidence to take on their goal. Ask yourself though, when will you become confident to take on your goal? You need to get out there, believe in yourself and have the confidence to do it, in order to achieve it.

Confidence is the knowing and belief that your goals and actions are completely achievable.

Challenge yourself and change your world

My advice is:

Take goal action, as once you get going you won't stop, and as long as you believe in yourself, you WILL achieve your goal.

Don't back down when the going gets tough, push through it.

Understand what your end goal is.

Know that successful people set goals.

If your goal doesn't challenge you, it won't change you to take action.

It's important and essential to set goals in life, be it personal or professional goals.

Those who do set goals end up creating a real reason to achieve them.

Don't settle for average in this life.

Don't accept failure in this life.

Challenge your own best at all times.

Live out your purpose in this life with zero excuses.

Ask yourself what the reason is, why you wake up each day.

Find your why.

Ask yourself, "Today, how can I be the best I can be?"

Be 100% committed to your belief.

Be 100% determined to achieve your end goal.

Acknowledgements

Thanks to:

My family for putting up with me on all these crazy adventures.

My team; Ian White, Dan Walker and Michael Jorgeson. Thank you for your continued support throughout my barefoot challenge and thank you Ian for saving my ass on day 2.

Jo and Joe from JoJoe's Hair Salon. Your fundraising support has been amazing.

To Sean Conway. You Legend… you know why!

To Paul Burgum. Thanks for the inspiration.

To Christina Dove. Thanks for your continued inspiration.

To everyone who has supported me on Social Media over the years, I want to say a big thanks to you all.

To everyone who has donated to the charities I have supported on my adventures. Your donations have been greatly appreciated and will really help to make a difference. Thank you so much.

Special Thanks to:

Ian Glass Fitness for helping to get me "fit ready" for my barefoot adventure.

G Baxter Autobodies for helping to kit me out on this adventure with gear to protect me from the elements.

To Mark Payne for your support and for covering all of all my adventures in the Hartlepool Mail.

Jamie Boyle for your involvement with the promotion of this book. Thank You.

The Chris Lucas Trust

The Chris Lucas Trust was set up after teenager Chris's tragic death from rhabdomyosarcoma, a cancer that resembles muscle tissue in July 2000.

Chris' parents, Lynn and Lynn, have so far raised over £2 million for research into rhabdomyosarcoma at the Institute of Cancer Research (ICR) and continue to fundraise through flagship events such as the Great North Bike Ride, a yearly event that takes place each August Bank Holiday Sunday seeing 2000 cyclists all ride 60 miles down the beautiful coastline of Northumberland and finishing off at Tynemouth Priory, all with the same goal of raising as much money as possible for the research into childhood cancer.

Before being diagnosed in July 1997, Chris was a strong 15 year-old boy who played rugby, cricket and basketball. After twice coming back from the disease, achieving great GCSE results and starting a career in graphic design, the cancer finally took Chris after a three year battle.

The Chris Lucas Trust hopes to enable the rapid translation of new targeted therapies into the ICR clinic so that other families don't suffer the same fate.

Donations from the trust have already contributed to studies that found combining two separate molecularly targeted therapies could block processes driving growth in rhabdomyosarcoma, a major cause of cancer death in children and young people.

Chris' mum, Lynn, says: "The Chris Lucas Trust chose to support the ICR since we believe in their commitment to develop new drugs to help children and young adults suffering from cancer to live longer, and ultimately to find a cure for rhabdomyosarcoma. We recognised their expertise in

153

childhood cancer when we first sought advice about funding research."

Any parent would dread being told their child has cancer, something Lynne and her husband Lynn have sadly been through. A diagnosis of rhabdomyosarcoma is a truly devastating one as there are currently no effective targeted treatments for the aggressive form of this disease, however, children and teenagers with rhabdomyosarcoma could one day be offered more effective treatments thanks to scientists funded by the Chris Lucas Trust who are developing treatments targeted at the specific genetic flaws driving the growth of these deadly tumours.

You can find out more about the Chris Lucas Trust by heading over to their website and social media pages.

www.chrislucastrust.com

https://www.facebook.com/Chris-Lucas-Trust-Rhabdomyosarcoma-Appeal-109434065770066/

https://twitter.com/chrislucastrust

Charity Number: 1085775

Hartlepool Ambulance Charity

Hartlepool Ambulance Charity (HAC) was set up in 2018 with the intention of helping to save local lives in Hartlepool and surrounding areas by empowering residents with first aid training skills, a defibrillator rollout scheme and providing ambulance support across the town.

Fundraising efforts allow Hartlepool Ambulance Charity to collectively provide these lifesaving public defibrillators, first aid training opportunities for town residents of all ages, help train equip and retain volunteer medics and responders and also provides ambulances and ambulance pedal cycles.

All ambulance charity workers are volunteers, giving their time and skills to help save local lives in their community.

Hartlepool Ambulance Charity also provide a wide range of medical cover at events around the region, from big town events to a smaller presence at low key functions.

Volunteers come from all walks of life and from all experience levels, with team members having backgrounds in Police, Search and Rescue, Paramedic and other ambulance service backgrounds along with home grown first aiders from within the charity.

You can find out more about Hartlepool Ambulance Charity by heading over to their website and social media pages.

https://www.hartlepoolambulance.co.uk

https://www.facebook.com/hartlepoolambulance/

https://twitter.com/HpoolAmbulance

Charity Number: 117833

Remember...

Anything is possible!

Keep up to date with Paul's adventures

www.paulsuggitt.com

@ultraadventurer

Also available from Warcry Publishing

Lee Duffy: The Whole of the Moon

ISBN: 978-1-9125430-7-6

A book which has taken over 25 years to arrive. The definitive story of the man who held an eight year reign of terror over the town of Middlesbrough. Containing many first-hand and previously unheard accounts from some of Duffy's closest friends and associates.

Lee Duffy 'The Whole of the Moon' Documentary DVD

August 25th 1991 at 3.55am saw the inevitable end to Lee Duffy's life. Everyone knew Lee's existence on this planet would be brief, including Lee and his Mother but the news Teesside was waking up to that gloriously sunny morning would rock it to its foundations. Lee has been gone now more years than he was alive although he is still spoken of as if he was here yesterday. Lee Duffy was arguably Teesside's most prolific criminal but where did his violent side stem from? Was he a figure of evil or misunderstood?

Terry Dicko: The Madness Continues

ISBN: 978-1-9125432-7-4

What's it about? Well the clues in the name... More bonkers tales of the funny man from Teesside coming this Halloween. The eagerly anticipated follow up to Laughter, Madness & Mayhem.